HERPES

HERPES

―――

ALAN E.
NOURSE, M.D.

FRANKLIN WATTS
NEW YORK ▪ LONDON ▪ TORONTO ▪ SYDNEY ▪ 1985
AN IMPACT BOOK

Photographs courtesy of: Centers for Disease Control, Atlanta, Georgia: pp. 13, 14, 15, 27 (top and bottom); Burroughs Wellcome Company: pp. 21, 42.

Library of Congress Cataloging in Publication Data
Nourse, Alan Edward.
Herpes.

(An Impact book)
Includes index.
Summary: Discusses the characteristics of one of the most rapidly increasing sexually transmitted diseases and describes its symptoms and effects. Also provides some suggestions for curbing its spread.
1. Herpes genitalis—Juvenile literature.
[1. Herpes genitalis. 2. Venereal diseases]
I. Title. [DNLM: 1. Herpes Genitalis—popular works.
WC 578 N933h]
RC147.H6N68 1985   616.95′1   85-5152
ISBN 0-531-10069-3

CONTENTS

HERPES

1

THE
HERPES
GANG

Ahundred years ago on the American frontier, when the Wild West was really wild, whole regions were terrorized by gangs of marauding outlaws who took what they wanted and never stopped to ask questions. Some of those bandit gangs went down in history—Quantrill and his raiders, Jesse James and his brother Frank, the Dalton boys, and the Younger brothers and their followers, to name just a few.

None of these bandits were up to any good at all. They accomplished nothing for anyone but themselves. They would appear out of nowhere to hold up stagecoaches, rob mail trains, stick up banks, or burn down whole towns, shooting anyone who tried to interfere with them and evading all attempts at law enforcement.

Today, of course, those Wild West bandits are a thing of the past. But now we are at the mercy of another kind of outlaw marauder. These modern-day bandit gangs are different from the Wild West outlaws of the past, for they are made up of microbes in the world around us. Yet they share many of the same characteristics of Quantrill's Raiders or the James brothers. Some of these villains—the Streptococcus Gang, the Staphylococcus Gang, or the Salmonella Gang, for example—are familiar to almost everyone. Practically everyone reading this book has tangled with these gangs of outlaw organisms at one time or another, and knows something about them. But one of the most active and troublesome of all these gangs of microbes—the Herpes Gang—is not nearly so well known to most people.

THE MICROBES AROUND US

Although you might never guess it just to look around, we live in a world teeming with tiny living entities called *microorgan-*

isms or microbes, all so very small that we must use powerful microscopes to see them. These microbes cover our skin, hair, and clothing. They are on the surface of every object that we touch, in the water we drink, and floating around in the air we breathe.

One large group of these microbes are tiny, one-celled organisms called *bacteria.* Oddly enough, most bacteria are extremely beneficial to humankind. In the soil they capture nitrogen from the air and supply it to growing plants in the form of vital nutrients. Elsewhere in the earth they help decay dead vegetation and turn it back into soil. On the surface of our bodies some bacteria help us to develop local immunity, or protection, against internal invasion by more deadly microbes. In the human intestinal tract these beneficial bacteria help prepare our body wastes for disposal. But a few groups or "gangs" of bacteria cause nothing but trouble. The Streptococcus Gang, for example, can cause severe throat infections, scarlet fever, or blood poisoning, and produce poisonous by-products that can lead to dangerous diseases such as rheumatic fever or nephritis (kidney damage). The Salmonella Gang can cause diseases in the intestines ranging all the way from a disabling travelers' diarrhea to deadly typhoid fever. The Staphylococcus Gang can cause skin infections ranging from sties to boils to serious wound infections. Other bacteria cause pinkeye, diphtheria, gangrene, and tuberculosis.

Doctors use the word *pathogenic* (from Greek words meaning "causing suffering") to describe these disease-causing bacteria, and in many ways these organisms behave very much like our Wild West bandits. They serve no useful purpose. They attack innocent people indiscriminately. They can cause severe disability and sometimes take lives, and some of them are even able to evade or escape the body's major "law enforcement" agency, the *immune system,* which is designed specifically to protect us from just such attacks. And some of these bacteria, which are ordinarily held in check by the body's immune system, can move in swiftly and cause damage or death the moment the immune system breaks down for some reason, as we will see in more detail later.

Two other groups of microbes that can behave like outlaws are the *protozoa*—tiny, one-celled animal organisms— and the *fungi*. Because many types of protozoan organisms thrive best in very warm climates, the diseases they cause are uncommon in the United States but cause enormous trouble in other parts of the world. Examples of these are *schistosomiasis*, an infection by a wormlike protozoal parasite that attacks millions of people in tropical areas, and *malaria*, a worldwide scourge in tropical and subtropical climates. Fungus infection can cause minor annoyances in the form of itchy ringworm of the scalp, athlete's foot, or severe infections of the lungs and other organs.

The most perplexing and troublesome of all the microbes, however, are the *viruses*—organisms so very tiny and so primitive that they can only live and reproduce inside living cells. Outside of the host cell, viruses are as inert and lifeless as salt crystals in a shaker. Indeed, a virus consists of little more than a tiny packet of hereditary material, DNA or RNA, wrapped up in a protein envelope. Only by forcing its way into a living cell and attaching its DNA or RNA to the hereditary material in the host cell can the virus "come to life" and begin commanding the cell to manufacture more virus particles.

Viruses are particularly unpleasant customers. Not one of them, to our knowledge, accomplishes anything useful to humankind. Many of them produce devastating diseases. Yellow fever virus and hepatitis B virus, for example, attack and destroy liver cells. The encephalitis virus can cause long-term damage to brain cells, leading to prolonged illness or even death. One large group of virus outlaws, the Influenza Gang, can cause worldwide epidemics of flu. The Rotavirus Gang has recently been discovered to cause many cases of severe summer diarrhea in infants and children. Other viruses cause such unpleasant diseases as rubeola (red measles), rubella (German measles), varicella (chicken pox), variola (smallpox), or poliomyelitis (polio).

Fortunately, our bodies are normally equipped with an elaborate defense system for fighting off most of these microbe invaders and protecting us from reinvasions. This is lucky for us, because we wouldn't be around long without such defenses. In most cases this body defense system, the immune system, does a highly effective job of fighting off virus marauders as well as other microbe invasions—but one particular band of outlaw viruses, the Herpes Gang, presents the immune system—and the human body—with some real problems. To better understand the very odd behavior of the Herpes Gang of viruses in general, and especially the ones responsible for genital herpes, we need to pause briefly for a closer look at the immune defense system and how it works.

FIGHTING OFF THE MICROBES

Whenever foreign invaders such as bacteria or viruses find entry into the body through a break in the skin or just by shouldering their way through moist mucous membranes lining such areas as the nose and throat, the intestinal tract, or the genital organs, they are met by a formidable first line of defense. Special kinds of white blood cells flock to the area of the invasion. Some of these cells, called *monocytes*, are circulating constantly in our blood stream. Others, called *macrophages* ("big eaters"), are constantly wandering on patrol through the tissues of the body. These wandering scavenger cells are both the front line soldiers and the garbage collectors of the body; they are programmed to set upon and devour virtually any kind of foreign substance they happen upon, and begin engulfing and digesting the invading microbes as fast as they can. In many cases these cells may succeed in stopping a foreign microbe invasion before it really gets started.

When that first line of defense is not enough, the body's immune system has even more powerful weapons with which to fight back a foreign invasion. From the beginning of life onward, cells in the body's bone marrow—the spongy red tissue in the ends of the long bones, packed into the thick bones of the pelvis, or in the interior of the ribs—is constantly manufacturing millions and millions of special small white blood cells called *lymphocytes.* Some of these lymphocytes, after they mature, take up residence in special tissues in the lymph glands located in the armpits, the groin, the lining of the intestine, or in organs such as the spleen; others travel to the thymus gland, a soft mass of glandular tissue located high up in the chest beneath the breastbone. Immunologists speak of the lymphocytes that mature in the bone marrow as B-lymphocytes or B-cells. Those that travel to the thymus gland are called T-lymphocytes or T-cells. The distinction is important, because the B-cells and the T-cells have quite different jobs to perform in the fight against foreign invaders.

Millions of the B-lymphocytes become, in effect, roving military police of the body, traveling by way of watery pathways known as *lymph channels* to the body's tissues far and wide in search of foreign invaders. B-cells have an uncanny ability to distinguish "self" from "not-self" substances that they encounter. That is, they can distinguish between the proteins, chemicals, and structures that properly "belong" as normal parts of the body and are therefore "okay," and other substances that have no business being in the body— foreign invaders of all kinds that are therefore perceived as "not-self" or "enemies." Every foreign microbe or cell or protein or chemical carries certain special surface markers called *antigens* that can give it away to the roving lymphocyte army. Once recognizing a "not-self" marker on an invading virus or on a cell that the virus has invaded, the roving lymphocytes sound the alarm to other B-lymphocytes, which immediately begin producing special "antidote protein" molecules known as *antibodies* to oppose the invading antigen. These specially designed antibodies then flood into the bloodstream and get to work counteracting the invading antigen.

Because the antibodies are carried in the blood to the invasion site and take actions to destroy the invader on their own, they are known as the body's *humoral* ("carried by the blood") immune response. Untold millions of these antibodies may be manufactured in a very short time, but their production and release into the bloodstream is very carefully and cleverly controlled by the body. At the beginning of the immune response, to make sure that the B-cells produce enough antibodies fast enough, certain of the T-cells act as "helper-lymphocytes" which stimulate or turn on the B-cells' antibody factories to produce antibodies at exceptionally high gear. But when the microbe invasion has been squelched and brought under control, to make sure that these turned-on B-cells don't keep on producing far too many antibodies, other T-cells act as "suppressor-lymphocytes" to slow down production and put out the fire before it begins to do possible damage.

In addition, other T-lymphocytes go forth to the site of the battle much as we might send destroyers to the center of a naval fray, and they act directly as "killer cells" to destroy the foreign invader. In accomplishing this task the killer T-cells work in close coordination with other white blood cells known as *granulocytes* to destroy and mop up the invasion. This wing of the body's immune defense system is sometimes spoken of as the *cellular* part of the immune system. Actually, however, this cellular immune response and the humoral immune response conducted by the antibodies do not really work independently at all. They work in close coordination, and working together they provide an integrated and complex defense system that is not only capable of fighting off invasion by bacteria but is especially effective in preventing the spread of virus invaders—at least in most cases.

Our immune response system has one other remarkable ability that is vital to the long-term protection of our bodies: *it remembers what happened before* and can gear up our defenses against a reinvasion very swiftly indeed. Our protection against a virus that is invading our bodies for the first time does not end when that first virus invasion is opposed by the defense system and the virus thrown out. If that foreign invader's antigen ever again appears in the body, even months or years later, the immune system remains alert and geared up for almost instant response. The invading antigen will be recognized immediately. Some of the opposing antibodies will still be circulating in the bloodstream and other elements of the immune system will swing into instant action. As a result, the re-invading organism may not even get a foothold at all before it is wiped out, or if it does, it will be fought back far more swiftly and effectively than the first time, so that any resulting illness is likely to be much less severe.

It is this remarkable action of the immune system that protects us from contracting serious virus diseases like measles or yellow fever or hepatitis B over and over again. By the time a first infection by one of these marauders has been beaten down, the body has developed a lasting *immunity* to that microbe; the immune system remains ready and waiting to deal swiftly with future attacks so that a second invasion cannot succeed. What is more, by taking advantage of this behavior of the immune system, scientists have been able to develop protective vaccines against many virus infections so the body can be protected in advance, and even a first infection cannot get started. For example, very young children can be given a polio vaccine made up of polio viruses that have been weakened, or *attenuated*, in the laboratory to the point that they cannot cause active polio infection. Given this vaccine long before they have had any contact with dangerous disease-causing polio viruses, their immune systems can be stimulated to make armies of polio antibodies well in advance of a real invasion. Should these vaccinated children contact dangerous polio viruses later, their polio antibody armies are ready and waiting to prevent them from developing this deadly disease.

The importance of vaccination as a defense against dangerous infections cannot be overexaggerated. Widespread vaccination against smallpox throughout the world over the years has been instrumental in wiping this fatal disease off the face of the earth, probably permanently, and a similar countdown against red measles is in progress right now. Thanks to the measles vaccine, scientists believe that within a few years measles can also be eradicated. Probably the only way we will ever be able to rid the world of a widespread killer disease like malaria will be through the use of a very inexpensive and widely available effective vaccine—but so far no one has succeeded in developing a vaccine against this protozoal infection.

THE HERPES GANG

Effective as the immune system may be in protecting us against multitudes of bacterial and viral invaders, it is not always completely successful. There is one gang of viruses in particular—the so-called *herpes viruses*—that have proven themselves singularly adept in evading and escaping the attacks of the immune system so that they can cause human beings prolonged and continuing trouble. Until very recently almost nobody except doctors had ever even heard of this unpleasant family of viruses, and this is not surprising. Although all these herpes viruses cause human infections, the infections they cause have seemed, in the past, relatively minor and not very important. It is only in recent years, as *virologists* (scientists specializing in the study of viruses) have begun to learn more about this gang of virus marauders, that they have come to realize that these herpes viruses are very nasty customers indeed.

For one thing, the infections that the herpes viruses cause are extremely widespread. Practically everybody gets at least one herpes infection (varicella, commonly known as chicken pox) before they reach the age of ten, and literally millions of people may have two or three *different* herpes infections that we know of (and perhaps one or two more that we don't know much about) before the age of forty. For another thing, the herpes viruses are especially skillful in hiding away in various nooks and crannies of the body after causing an infection and thus effectively escaping from the body's natural immune defense system. This means that once these viruses invade the body they are there to stay; there is no good way to get rid of them. And indeed, the more virologists learn about certain of the herpes viruses, the more they suspect that some of them may be able to tamper with various parts of the immune system so that the system doesn't work as effectively as it should, thus making it possible for the herpes viruses to escape and survive more readily.

But above all, there has recently been great concern about the marked increase in one of the herpes infections in particular. This infection is called *genital herpes* because the virus attacks cells in the male and female genital areas, causing painful, recurrent sores to occur in the region. Because this particular infection has proven to be extremely communicable and because no known antibiotic or other medicine will cure it, in recent years it has become one of the most rapidly increasing of all sexually transmitted diseases, severely disrupting the sex life and interpersonal relations of millions of people.

What exactly are these herpes viruses? There are five major members of the herpes family. All of this gang are bad characters, but some are a little worse than others. We will be looking at each one of them in more detail later in the book, but here is a brief roundup to help get us oriented.

The first, and probably the most familiar, is the *herpes zoster virus* (HZV), also sometimes known as the *varicella zoster virus.* You may not be familiar with its name, but just about everyone is familiar with its effects, because this is the virus that causes chicken pox, more properly known as *varicella.* Later in life HZV can emerge from hiding in the body and cause a second, very painful kind of skin infection known as *shingles.*

Another prominent member of the Herpes Gang is the Epstein-Barr virus (EBV), named after English virologists M. A. Epstein and Y. M. Barr, who first discovered it in 1964. Today we know that the Epstein-Barr virus is the cause of a tenacious, feverish infection known as *infectious mononucleosis,* which commonly strikes teen-agers and young people.

Cytomegalovirus (CMV) is a third member of the Herpes Gang—a far more obscure member than the others and one that scientists have only recently begun to learn very much about. This virus causes urinary and genital infections in adults and sometimes very severe skin infections in children. It was once thought that this virus mainly threatened children who were born with poor immune defenses, but today we suspect that CMV actually infects people far more widely than anyone had originally suspected. It is also recognized as a special threat to people of all ages whose immune systems are not working properly for one reason or another—people who have had their immune systems purposely depressed following an organ transplant operation, for example, or damaged by drugs they have received for treatment of cancer.

The last two viruses in the Herpes Gang—the two that people today are most concerned with—are the Simplex Twins, *herpes simplex virus #1* (HSV-1) and *herpes simplex virus #2* (HSV-2). These two beauties are so extremely sim-

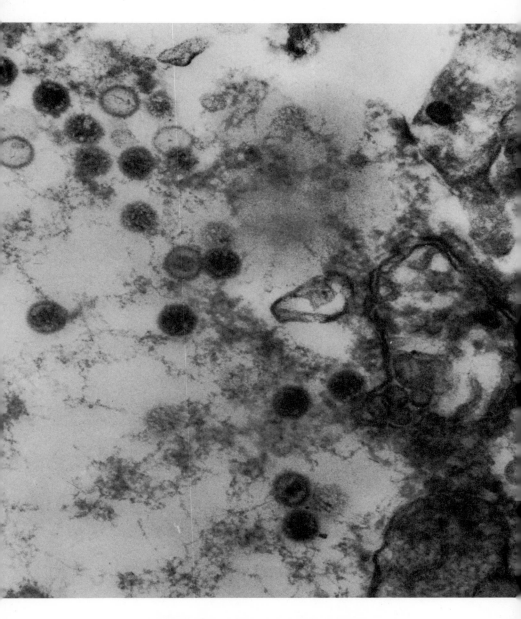

The Epstein-Barr virus as seen through
an electron microscope

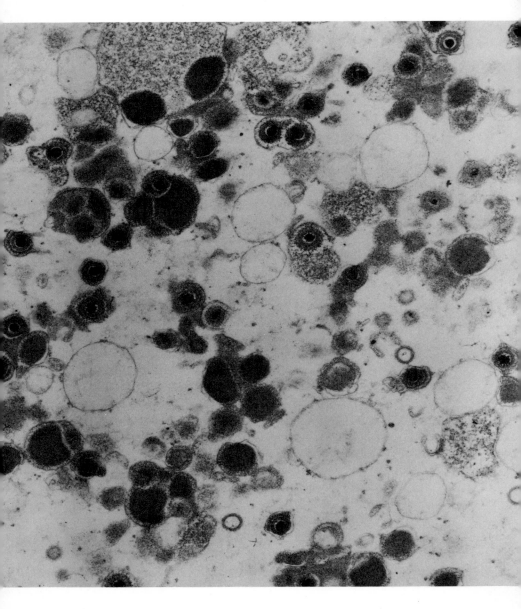

Above: *Cytomegalovirus (CMV) is a threat to people whose immune systems are not working properly.*
Opposite: *Various forms of herpes simplex virus*

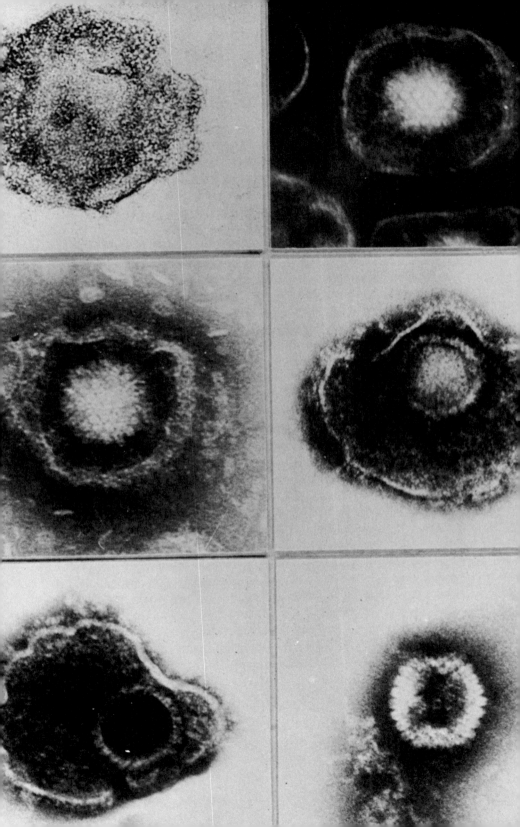

ilar in structure and appearance that only complicated laboratory tests can tell them apart, and both can cause thoroughly unpleasant infections in cells just below the surface layer of the skin. For years HSV-1 has been associated with cold sores or fever blisters—unsightly, painful, blistery sores that occur characteristically around the corners of the lips or nostrils. HSV-2 causes similar painful, blistery, ulcerated sores on the genital organs, especially on the penis of the male or the labia of the female. It is this infection, known today as genital herpes, that has come to cause so much distress and trouble in our time.

2

GENITAL HERPES: WHAT IS IT?

Some viruses can cause a lot more trouble than others. Some, for example, just aren't around in very great numbers so relatively few people are ever affected by them—the yellow fever virus, for example. Others, like the multitudes of common cold viruses or some intestinal viruses, are more a nuisance than a threat; they cause only mild upper respiratory or intestinal symptoms that last just a few days before the body's immune system succeeds in throwing them out and setting up immune barriers so that they can't come back again.

Other viruses, on the other hand, find ways to evade our immune defenses in some way. Such viruses can cause prolonged and highly distressing infections when they first invade the body, and then set up permanent housekeeping in places where the immune system cannot get at them. Such viruses don't necessarily have to be deadly, or bring about life-threatening diseases, in order to cause serious trouble for the human being who contracts them.

If we were to think of the most troublesome and annoying such virus imaginable, we would first think of one that was widely distributed, so that a great many people came in contact with it. Second, we would think of one that was highly infectious—that is, easily transmitted from one person to another. It would cause an unpleasant, painful, and prolonged infection for which there was no good treatment or cure and which would tend to recur again and again in spite of our body's best efforts to prevent recurrent infection. And finally, this virus would have some really effective way to hide from the body's immune system so that once it got well established there would be no good way for the body to get rid of it—ever.

This very unpleasant virus we have just pictured is, in fact, a perfect match for two of the Herpes Gang of viruses we spoke of in the last chapter—the Herpes Simplex Twins, herpes simplex virus #1 and herpes simplex virus #2.

These two viruses are, to all intents and purposes, identical twins. They can only be told apart by means of sophisticated laboratory tests or from the part of the body they most commonly attack. When viewed under the electron microscope they both look like many-sided, armor-clad space stations out of *Star Wars*, with spikes sticking out on all sides. This formidable-looking surface is actually an envelope of protein which surrounds the virus's vital inner core of genetic material, a twisted strand of a substance called deoxyribonucleic acid, more commonly known as DNA. It is this DNA that enables these virus particles to take control over the human cells that they invade.

On their own, these herpes viruses are quite inert and helpless. Outside a living cell they cannot grow or reproduce. It is only when a herpes virus particle has forced its way into a living cell—in this case, a cell located just under the surface layer of the skin—that it can come "alive" and spring into action, taking control of the cell's normal chemical factory and forcing the cell to manufacture more virus particles, which can then go on to invade other cells in the region.

Such an infection by a herpes simplex virus is called a *primary infection* when it is the first time that a person has been invaded by the virus. The end result of the primary infection depends in part upon which of the Herpes Simplex Twins is involved and what part of the body is attacked.

HSV-1 AND COLD SORES

In the case of HSV-1, the favorite site of invasion is one of the delicate areas of the face, most often at the corner of the lips or at the edge of a nostril. The virus may get inside the body through a tiny cut or scrape in the skin, or even directly

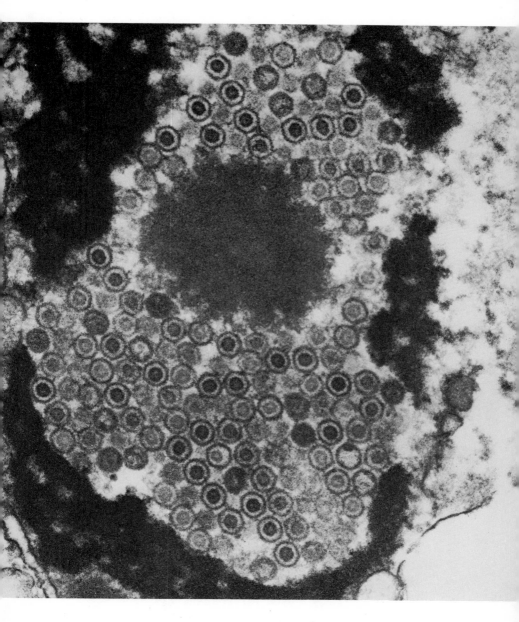

*An electron micrograph of a cell
invaded by herpes virus*

through the moist mucous membrane of the lip or nostril. The first evidence of infection is an intense irritation or itching and the reddening of the skin in the invaded area. Next, a group of small, itchy, fluid-filled blisters or *vesicles* appear. Very soon these vesicles run together and the blisters break to form a raw open sore which is quickly coated with a brownish crust.

This sore, which doctors speak of as a *lesion*, is now a typical "cold sore" or "fever blister." Neither of these common names for a herpes simplex lesion on the face is quite accurate. As far as we know the sores have nothing whatever to do with a head cold and they do not, as some people believe, occur only when a person has a fever. In some cases, however, a person may develop a slight fever and feel generally achy and sick for a day or so when the infection first begins.

Until very recently there was nothing at all you could do after a cold sore developed but wait for it to go away. From the time the blisters first appear until the crusted-over lesion is completely healed—a period of roughly two to three weeks—the cold sore will be teeming with HSV-1 viruses and the infection can easily be transmitted to another person, either by direct contact such as hugging, kissing, and shaking hands, or on washcloths, and so forth. After about ten days to two weeks the lesion will begin to shrink and dry up all by itself—sooner if a patient is treated with the new anti-virus antibiotic *acyclovir*, as we will see later—and presently it will heal without any scar or any other evidence that it was ever there.

That is not the end of the story, however. Even though the primary infection has healed, the virus particles are not dead, nor have they been eradicated from the body. Although the body's immune defense system has mounted a vigorous battle against the invading herpes simplex virus, that battle is not 100 percent effective in getting rid of the virus, for reasons that nobody understands. During the healing phase of the HSV-1 infection, these viruses, still very much alive, travel up nerve fibers and find a safe haven in small clusters of nerve cells called *ganglions* located close to the spinal cord. Inside these nerve ganglions, safe from further attack by the body's immune system, the viruses can lie dormant or "sleeping" for weeks or months, even years, without showing any sign that they are there. Then, sooner or later, again for reasons nobody yet understands, something happens to reawaken these same viruses and stimulate them into action.

Once reawakened, these herpes viruses travel back down the nerve fibers to areas close to where the primary infection occurred and cause a *recurrent* or *secondary* infection to begin. Once again itchy, blistery sores appear on the skin. Once again multitudes of active viruses are produced so that the infection can be transmitted to other people. In fact, about the only difference that might be observed between a primary infection and a recurrent or secondary infection is that the recurrent infection may not be quite as severe as the primary and may not take quite so long to heal.

Nobody knows just what may trigger the chain of events that leads to a recurrent infection. Perhaps some small injury to the skin area may stimulate it. Maybe a fever from another cause actually *does* have something to do with it. More likely, however, there may be a temporary weakening of the body's immune defense system that allows the dormant virus to come out of hiding. And in fact, some very recent scientific studies have suggested that the dormant herpes virus itself may cause a temporary breakdown of part of the immune system which allows the recurrent infection to occur. This might explain why one person whose immune system is in tip-top shape and whose body is in good physical condition may go for years without a recurrence of a herpes simplex infection, while another person whose immune system is already beaten down by some other kind of illness and who is not in good physical condition has recurrence after recurrence for no apparent reason. Whatever the true reason, one thing is sure: The immune defenses that helped the body fight down the primary infection didn't do a very good job of getting rid of this virus. It had just retired into its nerve cell hideout until something allowed it to come out again.

Virologists today believe that herpes simplex virus #1, once entrenched in the body by means of a primary infection, probably stays around for the rest of the person's life, ready at any time to cause a recurrent infection in spite of the immune system's best efforts to get rid of it. And unfortunately, this same characteristic of staying around forever is shared by HSV-1's identical twin, HSV-2.

HSV-2 AND GENITAL HERPES

Until recent years, hardly anybody except doctors had ever even heard of a sexually transmitted disease called genital herpes. Of course this disease existed years ago—but nobody talked about it very much. As few as ten years ago it was comparatively uncommon, and many of the people who came down with it didn't have the slightest idea what it was and in any event didn't see a doctor about it.

In the last ten years, however, the whole picture has changed. Partly because of far-reaching changes in people's sexual habits and practices in recent years, genital herpes has become increasingly prevalent. Today it is by far the fastest-spreading sexually transmitted disease in the country. Public health authorities estimate that some twenty million people in this country have genital herpes today, with approximately five hundred thousand new cases being added every year. Until some way is found to destroy the tenacious virus that causes this disease, the plain fact is that virtually every person who contracts genital herpes continues to harbor the living virus in his or her body for many years, perhaps for a lifetime.

In most cases the genital herpes infection is caused by the HSV-2 virus. However, at several treatment clinics where the viruses causing new infections are cultured and identified, as many as 10 percent of all new genital herpes infections appear to be caused by HSV-1 virus. In either case the virus is passed from an infected person to a noninfected person by means of sexual contact. Almost any kind of skin-to-skin sexual contact can do it—full or complete sexual intercourse isn't necessary. Some medical authorities believe that the great increase in genital herpes in recent years is a result of an increase in oral-genital sexual practices, and that many genital herpes infections caused by HSV-1 virus are in fact transmitted from active cold sores. There have also been a few reports of genital herpes arising as a result of contact with contaminated external objects such as toilet seats. And indeed, recent scientific studies have demonstrated that the herpes simplex viruses can remain alive and actively infective on a hard, dry external surface such as a toilet seat for a matter of several hours. Regardless of this, however, most doctors believe that this means of transmission of genital herpes is extremely uncommon and that virtually all cases arise from direct sexual contact.

In the genital area the virus can find entry anywhere that the skin is scraped or abraded, or may even penetrate through unbroken skin in the delicate, moist mucous membrane of the region. Thus in some cases genital herpes lesions can appear on the skin on the inside of the thigh or on the groin region, but in most cases the virus prefers to invade the delicate skin of the external genital organs proper—on the labia or at the entry to the vagina in the female, or on the skin of the penis, or foreskin, in the male.

The first evidence of an initial or primary infection appears about five days after sexual contact, in the form of one or more clusters of small, raised, reddened, itchy pimples. Within a few hours, more of these pimples develop and become patches of fluid-filled blisters or vesicles which become progressively more painful. In a day or so these vesicles break down, leaving raw, moist, painful open sores. At the same time in women, the virus has in most cases also invaded the surface cells of the *cervix*—the lower end of the uterus where it connects with the vagina. Since this area has very few pain-sensitive nerves, most women are not aware of this interior herpes infection. If, however, the virus also finds its way into the *urethra*—the tube that carries urine from the bladder to the outside—there may be burning pain at urination during this stage of the infection. The male may also have invasion of the urethra with resultant pain and burning on urination.

It is at this point in the infection that genital herpes is at the height of its infectivity, because the external sores in both male and female and the infection of the cervix in the female are teeming with virus particles. Doctors would say that the infected person is "shedding virus" so the infection can easily be passed from one person to another at this point by sexual contact. A primary infection of genital herpes will remain in this painful, open infectious state for about two weeks. In addition to the local genital symptoms described above, about four out of ten persons with a first or primary infection will have some general body symptoms as well. Some people may have a slight fever for two or three days, or suffer from malaise (a vague feeling of being ill). Others may have muscle aching in the back, hips, or legs. These so-called systemic symptoms tend to clear up in two or three days. At the end of two weeks the lesions in the genital area begin to heal by themselves if no treatment has been started to speed the healing. The healing phase takes another ten or eleven days, and at the end of this time the sores will be healed and the active virus gone. In other words, about three and one-half to four weeks after the very first symptoms appeared, the infected person will no longer be shedding virus and will no longer transmit the infection to other per-

FEMALE PELVIS

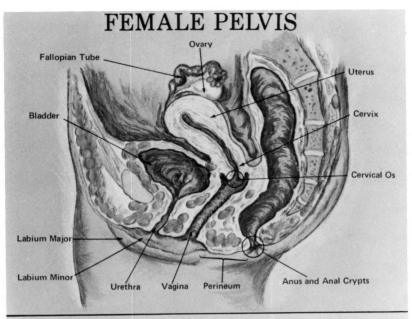

Ovary

Fallopian Tube

Uterus

Bladder

Cervix

Cervical Os

Labium Major

Labium Minor

Urethra   Vagina   Perineum

Anus and Anal Crypts

MALE GENITO-URINARY TRACT

Bladder   Vas deferens

Rectum

Prostate Gland

Urethra

Anus and Anal Crypts

Foreskin

Glans   Testis   Epididymis

sons through sexual contact—at least not for the time being.

RECURRENT GENITAL
HERPES INFECTION

Unfortunately, the healing of a primary genital herpes infection does not mean that the virus is destroyed or the infection cured. Like HSV-1, HSV-2 retreats up nerve fibers and finds a safe harbor in ganglion nerve cells that are located in small clusters near the spine. There the virus becomes dormant for a period of time. In fact, in some cases the virus may remain dormant forever; there are some people, once the primary infection is healed, who never have another sign of genital herpes for the rest of their lives.

According to recent estimates, about 10 to 15 percent of genital herpes victims fall into this fortunate group—they neither have recurring infection nor do they pass the infection on to others once the primary infection has completely healed.

For those who are not so lucky, the story is quite different. Some weeks, months, or even years after the primary infection has settled down, the virus that is hiding in the nerve ganglia becomes reactivated, moves back down the nerves to the skin area of the genital region and causes recurrent episodes of infection. This means that a person who is once infected with genital herpes stands a very good chance of having at least one recurrent attack, and a great many may have repeated attacks occurring over and over, for no apparent reason, whether there is any sexual activity or not, for many years.

The recurrent infections differ from the primary infection in several ways. Perhaps the best thing that can be said about a recurrent infection is that it is not likely to be as severe and prolonged as the primary infection. In most cases, for example, a recurrent infection will not be as painful as a primary; there may be only a few vesicles which form and then develop into one or two open sores. Virus shedding and infectivity are both present during an acute recurrence, but the recurrent infection tends to remain active only for about three or four days and then heal in the course of another week, so that it may be completely over in nine to ten days from the beginning of symptoms.

Furthermore, unlike the primary infection which comes on quite suddenly and without warning, a person often has a warning that a recurrent infection is about to start. This warning, which may come anywhere from two hours to two days before the first visible sign of the infection, consists of an itching or tingling sensation in the surface of the genital area where the vesicles are going to appear, and may be accompanied by an aching in the back, buttocks, or leg—the kind of pain doctors call *neuralgia* or "nerve pain." Since these warning symptoms usually turn up before a person has begun to become actively infective from the recurrence, it is often possible to take heed of the warning (knowing what is coming) and avoid sexual contact with anyone in sufficient time to avoid passing the infection on to another person during the recurrence.

How often are recurrent infections likely to occur among people who have them? No one can really say for sure, at least not yet. One major survey of six thousand people with genital herpes found that people averaged between five and eight recurrences per year—but the people in that survey were all individuals who were having a great deal of trouble with genital herpes. There may well be multitudes of others who have only one or two recurrences per year, or some, as we have seen, who have recurrences even more rarely than that, or none at all. Only further study of this disease will tell us the answer to this question, and since recurrences seem to depend at least partly on highly individual health factors such as the state of a person's resistance or the behavior of his or her immune system, there may never be any way to predict in advance which persons with genital herpes will have a great deal of trouble with recurrences and which ones will have relatively little trouble.

Who is likely to get a genital herpes infection? The problem is finding anyone who is *not* at risk of contracting this infection if exposed to it. The high incidence of primary infection begins to appear at the age at which young people become sexually active—around age twelve on up—and continues appearing into young adulthood. The plain fact is that anyone who engages in sexual contact with another person, whether of the same sex or the opposite sex, is at risk. True enough, there are some commonsense ways that the risk can be substantially reduced, as we will see in the next chapter, but the risk exists wherever there is sexual activity. Even newborn babies are at risk of developing herpes simplex infections, and this is one of the more ominous complications of genital herpes in young women of childbearing age. It has been found that a woman who has active, contagious genital herpes when she is about to have a baby runs an exceptionally high risk of transmitting that infection to her baby at the time of delivery—and of all babies infected in this way, about half of them die of the infection.

The reason for this is very simple: Newborn babies have very poorly developed immune protective systems, so they have almost no natural defense against the invasion of the herpes simplex virus at the time of birth. Consequently, the herpes lesions may appear and spread all over the baby's body in such an overwhelming infection that the infant cannot survive. Fortunately, this kind of disaster can usually be avoided today. Studies have shown that if a genital herpes infection is not active—that is, if it is in the dormant stage—when the time comes for a woman to deliver a baby, normal delivery is safe for the child. But if the infection has been active (therefore contagious) within two weeks or so of anticipated delivery time, or is still active, whether a primary infection or a recurrent infection, then the baby must be delivered surgically by Caesarean section to avoid possible contact with the genital herpes virus.

This means that the pregnant woman with genital herpes must be closely observed during the last third of her pregnancy and have regular laboratory tests and virus cultures at weekly intervals to determine whether the infection is active as delivery time approaches. By following this procedure the attending doctor can be prepared to go either way—Caesarean section or normal delivery—depending upon whether the mother's infection is active or inactive at delivery time, and thereby eliminate the risk of exposing a newborn baby to this dangerous virus.

Women must be concerned with one other possible complication of genital herpes that may affect them. For a long time doctors have suspected that the herpes simplex virus #2 may have some role to play in the long-term development of cancer of the cervix. So far no clear-cut proof has been found that this is so, and if there is some connection between the virus and developing cancer of the cervix no one is quite sure what it may be, but a number of things suggest the possibility. It is known, for example, that young women who become sexually active at a young age, or with a number of different partners, or both, seem to be more likely to develop this kind of cancer and to develop it at an earlier age than other women. These, of course, are the same young women who are the most likely to contract genital herpes, probably at an early age—and many young women who develop signs of cancer of the cervix at an early age have a history of genital herpes.

Fortunately, for most women, it is possible to detect cancer of the cervix in a very early stage when it can almost always be cured. A few surface cells scraped from the cervix in a doctor's office can be sent for a simple laboratory examination to detect the first signs of the cancer. This lab test is known as the Pap smear, named after its inventor, Dr. George Papanicolaou, a Greek-born American physician.

Since its first introduction in the early 1940s, the Pap smear has made it possible for doctors to detect most cancers of the cervix very early, and bring about an extremely sharp reduction in the death rate from this kind of cancer. Because of the possibility of a connection between genital herpes infections and the early development of cancer of the cervix, a woman who has this infection is usually advised to have a Pap smear examination done regularly, at least once a year, for her own protection.

Obviously genital herpes is a nasty customer. Now that people all over are suddenly becoming aware of it, lots of individuals are raising very sharp questions about it. "What can I do? How can I keep it from happening to *me*? What can I do if it *does* happen to me? Why can't it be cured?" These are perfectly legitimate questions, and fortunately there are some useful answers to some of them. Unfortunately, however, it is a plain fact that genital herpes, at the present time, is not yet *curable*. There is no way to eradicate it from the body the way doctors can eradicate a strep throat infection with penicillin. Genital herpes is, however, both *preventable* and *treatable*. In the next chapter we will see how the whole unhappy picture of genital herpes infection can be improved for those who have not yet become infected, and for those who have, by a combination of common sense, prevention measures, and modern treatment methods.

3

GENITAL HERPES: WHAT CAN YOU DO ABOUT IT?

Genital herpes is an especially difficult problem for modern adolescents and young adults. It is a thoroughly unpleasant virus infection that can cause serious pain and distress in anyone who has it. It can continue causing pain and distress for a long time. What is worse, it can interfere in a big way with social and sexual relationships of all kinds. Many victims become deeply depressed because the infection doesn't go away but keeps recurring over and over, seemingly endlessly. Many others feel that they have to back away from any kind of sexual relations once they have been discovered to have the infection; it makes them feel contaminated. And although it doesn't normally threaten the lives of mature people, it can certainly interfere seriously with a woman's childbearing experience and can threaten the lives of newborn babies. Last but not least, the infection is spreading rapidly in our society, affecting more and more people every year.

So everybody agrees that genital herpes is a mess—but what can be done about it? Many people have felt totally helpless in the face of this sexually transmitted epidemic. But the fact is that intelligent, alert people can do quite a bit to protect themselves against this plague. First of all, people can *learn all about the disease ahead of time* so that there aren't any big surprises or mysteries about what's going on. A great many people acquire genital herpes through plain, blind ignorance. You don't have to be one of them. Second, if you have never had the infection, you can consider taking some commonsense steps *to keep from getting it.* Third, if you do already have the infection, there are steps that you can take to *treat it* so that it doesn't last as long or cause as much trouble. At the same time, you can learn how to keep from spreading it to others. Fourth, if you already have the infection, or if somebody close to you does, there are things you can do *to keep the infection from wrecking your life* or causing the kind of psychological damage that some doctors believe can be the most devastating aspect of the disease. And finally, the time may well come when doctors can *cure* genital herpes or at least prevent it, although nobody yet knows how to do this. Let's consider each of these points in a little more detail.

FOREWARNED IS FOREARMED

There is nothing like knowing in advance that the roof of your house is getting ready to fall in on you. If you have some forewarning, you can make plans to get out from under it before it gives way. Many people every day avert disaster because they know in advance that the disaster is possible and prepare to avoid it.

Similarly, when you are concerned about a serious health hazard like genital herpes, which may well threaten *you,* it pays to know everything there is to know about the disease, right up front, in advance. Knowing and understanding all about the infection is the best possible first step there is in protecting yourself.

Twenty years ago this probably wouldn't have been possible in the case of a disease like genital herpes. After all, this infection is a sexually transmitted disease, and until very recently nobody talked about sexually transmitted diseases. Nobody published the plain facts about such diseases—certainly not for young people to read. Nobody taught anybody about them, and there were no books you could find to tell you the whole story.

Fortunately, times have changed. Today any person who wants to pay attention can easily learn all about genital herpes: what causes it, how it is spread from person to person, what the early symptoms are, what course the disease follows once it has been acquired, how to recognize it, and so on. With this kind of information at your command, you will have all the knowledge you need to be forewarned and armed in advance to protect yourself against infection by means of precautionary measures and plain common sense.

PREVENTION OF
GENITAL HERPES

Let's recognize at the start that there is no medicine that you can take to prevent genital herpes. There is no miraculous ointment that you can count on to protect you, no fully reliable "prophylaxis" (special preventive measures) such as can sometimes be used against other sexually transmitted diseases. And, as yet, there is no protective vaccine to prevent the infection. Any time the live HSV-2 virus comes in contact with susceptible cells in a person's genital area, that person is likely to sustain an infection. It follows that the most reliable way a person can guard against a genital herpes infection is to make sure that no live virus has the opportunity to come in contact with a susceptible area.

Avoidance of sexual contact altogether is one way to do this, and for many people it will seem by far the best way. If there isn't any sexual contact, there isn't going to be a genital herpes infection. Bear in mind, however, that "sexual contact" does *not* necessarily refer only to complete sexual intercourse. The infection can be transmitted just as readily by external sexual contact as by full intercourse; in fact, just about any form of genital sexual activity from heavy petting on can transmit the infection.

Nobody but the individual person can decide whether to avoid sexual contact or not in any given situation. But this is one place where foreknowledge of the possibility of infection can be a help. In circumstances in which there might otherwise seem to be no reason *not* to engage in sexual contact, a bell might go off somewhere in the mind saying, "Hold it! Wait a minute! What about this?" And this is precisely the kind of precautionary thought that everyone ought to be having these days.

Selectivity in sexual contacts is another way to reduce the chances of an unwanted infection. Essentially this means being very, very picky about persons one chooses to have sexual contact with. This is really nothing more than a matter of plain common sense. A young man or woman who has sexual relations with three or four different partners each week, each of whom is also having sexual contact with three or four different partners each week, is running a very *high risk* that one of these partners, sooner or later, is going to bring the genital herpes virus home to roost. On the other hand, a very close, loving couple who may have sexual contact with each other, perhaps frequently, but *never* with anyone else, are far less likely ever to acquire genital herpes.

In this area it is also important to bear in mind, as we saw in the last chapter, that not everyone who has a genital herpes infection is necessarily infective or able to transmit it all the time. Only a person with an active primary or recurrent infection that hasn't completely healed will transmit the virus. Obviously, then, it is extremely important that a person who has acquired this infection should be particularly careful to refrain from *any* sexual contact during any period when active lesions are present and not completely healed. This means backing away from sexual activity during any interval when the infection is active, whether you feel like it or not. This is a responsibility that is imposed upon a person along with the infection if the rampant spread of the disease is to be curbed in any way.

These, then, are rules for prevention which are simple and easy to understand. The fewer the sexual partners, the less risk of acquiring herpes. The more exclusive the sexual relations—that is, the more people who are *ruled out* of one's life as sexual partners—the less likely the infection will intervene, simply because there are fewer sources it might come from. And deliberately refraining from any sexual contact during the intervals when a person knows he or she has an infection that is currently active will protect the *other* person from unnecessary contact and infection.

Mechanical protection can limit the chances of contact with the virus. If the male partner wears a protective sheath or condom during sexual relations, the chances of direct contact with HSV-2 virus are greatly reduced. Of course this kind of protective device can also reduce chances of transmission of other sexually transmitted diseases such as gonorrhea or syphilis, and can reduce the chances of the female partner becoming pregnant. Unfortunately, the use of a condom is often bypassed because it tends to be clumsy and inconvenient—but all it really takes for this kind of protection to work is a willingness of both partners to put up with a minor annoyance in order to achieve a very considerable possible benefit.

Direct inquiry, one partner to the other, as to whether an active genital herpes infection might be present, makes an enormous amount of sense considering the extensive publicity there has been about this infection. It isn't as if it is something that neither partner has ever heard about. And in fact, direct inquiry has proven to be quite effective as a means of averting infection among mature, responsible people who recognize that genital herpes is a serious health threat that really should not be spread around if it can be avoided. The success of direct inquiry, of course, depends upon both partners' honesty and recognition of an obligation not to spread the disease, as we mentioned above. It also depends upon both partners' knowledge of when genital herpes is infective and when it is not. Genital herpes must be considered contagious from the time the first evidence of a lesion appears until healing is almost complete—a period of about three weeks from the beginning of symptoms in the case of a primary infection, or a few days less in the case of a recurrent infection. Knowing this, individuals can readily tell when, precisely, they should *avoid* sexual contact in order to reduce the risk of transmitting the infection to another; and during any such period of possible contagion, frank inquiry and disclosure can go a long way toward preventing the spread of this infection.

Vaccination against genital herpes would, of course, be the ideal preventative. It would be absolutely splendid if a person could have a vaccination sometime early in life and never again have to worry about ever contracting this disease. Unfortunately no such vaccine is yet available for general use. However, a number of research laboratories around the world are currently at work trying to develop just such a vaccine against genital herpes (see chapter 5 for more details), and there is a very real possibility that a safe, effective genital herpes vaccine may be developed in the not-too-distant future.

TREATING GENITAL HERPES

Preventive measures are by far the best possible answer to the herpes problem for those who use them effectively—and in time. But the fact is that many people *don't* know much about the disease and how it is transmitted. Even among those who do, there are a great many who don't or won't pay attention to the dangerous time when sexual contact must be avoided. Others are just very shortsighted and say to themselves, "I haven't gotten it yet, why should I start worrying now?" As a result, there is a huge reservoir of genital herpes virus being transferred from person to person, and anyone who is sexually active may well encounter it sooner or later and acquire the infection. For these people, the important question becomes, What can be done about it?

As we have already seen, at the present time there is nothing that anyone can do to *cure* genital herpes. The best that can be done is to *treat* it as effectively as possible to try to keep it under control and limit the problems that it can cause. Since the disease was first recognized, the main goal of treatment has been first, to quiet the active infection and encourage it to heal as quickly as possible; and second, to do whatever was possible to prevent recurrent infection.

Until recently there was very little that could be done to achieve even these modest treatment goals. There was no antibiotic drug capable of attacking the virus. A dozen different kinds of ointments were used on the genital herpes lesions in hopes of making them less painful, drying them up more quickly, or making them less infective, but nothing really helped very much. About all a person could do was to keep the active lesions clean and dry, avoid irritation from clothing or from sexual contact, and wait for them to go away.

Recently, however, there have been several major breakthroughs in treating genital herpes. For years virologists had been searching in vain for a safe, effective drug that might have some kind of virus-killing effect on the herpes simplex virus. Then in 1974 one pharmaceutical company, the Burroughs Wellcome Company, announced a major discovery: a new antibiotic drug developed in their laboratories that seemed able to attack the herpes simplex viruses in the place where they were doing the most harm—inside the infected cell itself.

This drug was called *acyclovir,* and the way it worked was unlike any other antibiotic drug ever discovered. Outside the infected cell this drug seemed to have no effect whatever against the herpes simplex viruses—the drug was in an inactive form. But once acyclovir molecules found their way into the interior of a virus-infected cell, a chemical known as an *enzyme,* produced by the viruses themselves, changed acyclovir into a different and active form of the drug. This active form of acyclovir, working inside the infected cell, then turned on the virus and prevented it from *replicating* or reproducing itself, thus halting the spread of the infection in its tracks.

After long years of testing to be sure that acyclovir had no dangerous side effects on people who used it—and to make sure that it really did help control genital herpes infec-

tion—the drug was finally approved for general use. In March of 1982 acyclovir (under the trade name of Zovirax) received approval from the Food and Drug Administration (FDA) for use in an ointment form against genital herpes and HSV-1 infections as well.

WHAT ACYCLOVIR DOES AND DOESN'T DO

Acyclovir did not prove to be a cure for genital herpes, as some had hoped it would be. It merely helped *control* the infection under certain circumstances and in certain ways. Acyclovir ointment didn't destroy the genital herpes virus, but it slowed down its reproduction and thus its ability to spread the infection. It didn't prevent recurrence of the infection, and it didn't do much good in treating a recurrence when it happened—at least in its original ointment form and applied to the surface of genital herpes lesions.

Acyclovir *does* help a good deal, however, in treating *primary* genital herpes infections, the very first attack a person has. Starting at the time when the first symptoms appear—a red, itchy, blistery rash that develops into open sores in the genital region, perhaps accompanied by fever, headache, or aching in the groin or leg—the drug in ointment form can be prescribed by a doctor to be applied to the surface of the developing lesion, and rubbed in well to penetrate the infected cells. This kind of local application of the drug to the infected area works best if it is done every three hours, six times a day, and continued for a period of seven days. Applying the ointment may not be very comfortable, because these

Acyclovir crystals magnified 5,200 times

lesions can be extremely tender and sore, but the treatment has definite benefits. In most cases acyclovir will reduce the length of time the primary sores remain open and active. It will reduce (but will not eliminate) the pain and itching. It will reduce the length of time that the sore is infective to others; and it will speed up the healing of the lesions. There is even some evidence that a primary infection promptly and thoroughly treated with the acyclovir ointment may be followed by fewer recurrent infections and that the recurrences may be farther apart—but this has not yet been definitely proven.

Unfortunately, experience with this drug in ointment form since its introduction in 1982 has shown that there is one important thing that it will *not* do: it will *not* have any significant, measurable effect on the severity and duration of recurrent infections. This has been a grave disappointment to physicians who were hoping that the acyclovir ointment would prove a good weapon against genital herpes any time it recurred. Nobody as yet knows precisely why the drug seems to have little or no effect on recurrent infections—it just doesn't seem to reach or affect the virus in these recurrent lesions the same way it does with the virus present in the primary infection.

One other problem has researchers worried about the use of acyclovir ointment. This is not a concern about dangeous side effects for the user—the drug has been thoroughly tested and no such bad side effects have appeared as yet. But some evidence suggests that the HSV viruses may be able to develop resistance against acyclovir, and that a low concentration of the drug such as is present in the ointment may actually encourage this to happen. We know that many bacteria have found ways to develop resistance to powerful antibiotics that have been used against them, and that it is often low dosages of these antibiotics that have allowed the bacteria to develop that resistance. In low dosage there just isn't enough antibiotic around to kill *all* the bacteria present, and the few that survive give rise to a new generation of bacteria that are able to resist the antibiotic's killing influence. This is one reason that many virologists are urging doctors who are treating genital herpes to reserve the acyclovir ointment *only* for use in primary infections, where it may do some good, but to refrain from using it to treat recurrent infections where it is largely ineffective anyway.

Certainly acyclovir is a step in the right direction. It does help control the severity and length of the primary infection. Some virologists, though, believed that this drug was far too inefficient in the ointment dosage form. Therefore, studies of the drug in pill form, to be taken by mouth, were begun. In 1985 the FDA approved this oral form of acyclovir as effective for reducing the frequency and severity of recurrent attacks of genital herpes. Other medical centers are studying an intravenous dosage form of the drug on the theory that this kind of dosage might bring more of the drug into contact with the infected cells all at one time. We will discuss some of the most recent findings of these studies, and the promise that they offer, in more detail in chapter 7.

Meanwhile, as the search for more effective antiviral drugs goes on, doctors have been working out ways to help protect pregnant women with genital herpes—and their babies. Today doctors are able to test infected mothers once a week during the last eight weeks of pregnancy in order to detect any sign of active virus activity. If these tests show no evidence of recurrent infection as the end of the pregnancy approaches, then doctors feel that normal delivery of the baby will be safe. But if any sign of virus activity is found close to delivery time, this is an indication that a Caesarean delivery will be safer for the baby. As time goes on and laboratories gain experience, this testing for virus activity becomes both more accurate and much more speedy than it used to be. Among the techniques that laboratories can use to detect virus activity are *virus cultures,* in which the mother's vaginal secretions can be inoculated into living cells in the laboratory in order to see if HSV viruses grow, and the Tzanck test, in which any growing and multiplying viruses present can be quickly detected. A very recent new "quick test" for herpes viruses developed by researchers with the support of the National Institutes of Health can detect the first sign of virus activity within twenty-four hours, and an even more speedy test, still under development, may reduce that time to as little as four and a half hours. These speedy tests are important not only to the infected mother but also to the possibly infected newborn baby; sometimes, despite all precautions, a newborn baby appears after delivery to be infected even though the mother had no apparent sign of viral activity at all just prior to delivery. In such a case swift positive diagnosis of the infection in the baby may be lifesaving, since treatment measures can be started without delay.

COPING WITH GENITAL HERPES

Obviously preventive measures against genital herpes leave much to be desired, and treatment procedures, at present, offer only limited help. So what can you do if you find you have contracted the infection? Faced with the problem of genital herpes, with its frequent recurrences and no prospect of a cure in sight, a great many people become extremely discouraged. In fact, according to Dr. Lawrence Corey of the University of Washington School of Medicine, a specialist in dealing with this disease, the major and most serious complication of recurrent genital herpes is the stigma and emotional distress of dealing with this chronic disease. Some people are terrified at the knowledge that they have developed the infection and feel that they have to totally rearrange their lives, especially their sexual lives. Others become deeply depressed at what they (incorrectly) assume to be the absolute hopelessness of it all. Perhaps worst of all, many are so panicked at the thought that they might have contracted genital herpes that they won't seek medical help at all to confirm or rule out the diagnosis and may spend months or years convinced that they have the infection when they actually don't, or pretending to themselves that they don't have the infection when they actually do. Finally, a great many feel the stigma of the disease very deeply and are too embarrassed to share the burden with anyone else or to seek any relief from the distress.

Certainly genital herpes is a discouraging condition to have to deal with—but it is not entirely the end of the world. Although it is a thoroughly unpleasant, recurring infection that is recognized by everyone as a sexually transmitted disease, it is not by any means the worst such disease that a person could contract. Genital herpes is not the terrible potential killer that syphilis is, nor the permanently crippling disease that gonorrhea can be, as we will see when we review these other sexually transmitted diseases in chapter 5. Unpleasant as genital herpes may be, people can and do live with it, and there is no reason that it should be allowed to ruin anyone's life. While it is true that the infection may be active part of the time, there is much of the time when it is not active. Nor is there any reason that it need be allowed to destroy or seriously alter one's sexual relationships, so long as you know enough about the disease to know when it is active. Certainly a person should avoid sexual contact during the few days of an active recurrence—but this does not necessarily mean one has to avoid closeness to a spouse or partner or friend during these periods.

There are several things that can help you deal more comfortably with the fact of having contracted genital herpes, depending upon your own individual situation. First, you can develop a frank and open contact with a trusted and sympathetic physician. This is not a time to be stumbling around in the dark. Anyone who even suspects that he or she might have contracted genital herpes should talk with a doctor who has had some experience dealing with the problem. Such a doctor may be a family practitioner that you already know or a completely different physician, perhaps a urologist in the case of a male patient, or a gynecologist (a specialist in women's diseases) in the case of a female. By now many major medical centers associated with medical colleges or universities, or large city medical clinics, have established special departments for dealing with genital herpes infections, staffed by the doctors in the community who have experience and know-how in dealing with the disease. (In many cities such special clinics may actually be carrying out research on the disease, so that members of the staff will be completely up-to-date on what is new.)

What can seeing a physician do for you? First, a doctor can help you determine for sure whether you actually have the infection or not. Second, assuming that the diagnosis is established, a doctor can help you become fully informed and educated about the nature of the infection and what it means to you—and what it doesn't mean. Third, a doctor can guide you in the best available treatment of either a primary or a recurrent infection, recommending what to do when or what forms of treatment not to bother with, based on the latest knowledge about the infection. And fourth, a doctor can keep you informed of the latest ongoing developments in the area of medical research in which new knowledge is being gathered every day.

In short, a doctor can provide the help that is available from modern medicine—but doctors' schedules are crowded, and the doctor may not be in a position to help you very much with the emotional, social, or sexual relationship problems you find yourself struggling with. For this reason, and especially for young people in their teens, it can be extremely important to find *some other kind of counselor* with whom to share and talk out the problems. For some young people who are lucky enough to have a warm, close, and trusting relationship with one or both parents, such parents are the obvious choice. For other young people for whom relations with parents are already filled with conflict, a parent might be a very bad choice. No one could possibly know better which choice would be best than you yourself. If you have a relationship with a parent that makes discussion of the problem seem like a good idea, probably the best possible approach is one of complete and total frankness; oddly enough, the degree of maturity that you show in bringing the problem to them may well have a great deal of influence on how they react to it and how much help and support they can provide. For those who feel that discussion with parents would *not* be a good choice, a counselor outside the family may offer an alternative. Many young people may already have formed a friendly and trusting relationship with a teacher, a guidance counselor or other school counselor, or a social worker connected with the school. Such persons may have time and willingness to help a person unload the worries, apprehensions, and problems that can go along with this infection. In any event, finding *someone* to confide in, if only a friend, may help you greatly in getting your thoughts together and realizing that this problem, while unpleasant and serious, is not a total disaster.

In addition, there are other sources of help you can call on. One organization, the American Social Health Association, is a national nonprofit health foundation that sponsors a membership program specifically organized and operated to assist herpes patients. This program, the Herpes Resource Center, has local chapters, known as HELP groups, in almost every large city. The organization provides educational literature about genital herpes and also provides members with a quarterly newsletter, operates a telephone hot line (1-800-227-8922) and organizes local self-help groups. For more information send a stamped, self-addressed envelope to:

HELP
P.O. Box 100
Palo Alto, California 94302

Finally, it is worth bearing in mind that a great deal of research is actively under way to solve today's problems with genital herpes, and this research will sooner or later bear fruit. Preventive vaccines, better dosage forms of acyclovir, new and different antiviral agents altogether—as we will see later, there is reason to hope that more effective ways of dealing with the disease will soon be appearing.

4

QUESTIONS AND ANSWERS ABOUT GENITAL HERPES

Any time a previously little-known infection appears and begins affecting large numbers of people, there are bound to be questions. Here are some of the questions that doctors are frequently asked about genital herpes:

Q. Is there any difference between males and females as far as susceptibility, frequency, or severity of genital herpes infections are concerned?

A. Not that anyone has been able to determine as yet. Both males and females seem to be equally susceptible to the infection, become infected with equal frequency when exposed to the virus, and suffer infections of equal severity—although the severity of infection may vary greatly from one individual to another. The infection may be more apparent in males than in females because their sexual organs are more exposed and the lesions therefore easier to see. Females have a relatively hidden genital area, the cervix or mouth of the uterus, which can be affected even when no external lesions are apparent. Thus it may be more likely for a woman to have a genital herpes infection without knowing it.

Q. Can a person have genital herpes without any symptoms at all?

A. This is perfectly possible, although not very common. In such a person the only way of detecting a genital herpes infection would be culturing the active virus from the genital tract or by detecting the virus, for example, on a Pap smear. Approximately two-thirds of all active genital herpes infections in females can be identified—or at least suspected—from a Pap smear examination. The other third of cases just don't show up this way. More commonly, there are people who contract such a mild case of genital herpes infection with so little evidence of it that they simply don't recognize it for what it is. Unfortunately, these people can be shedding just as much virus during the active phase of the disease, and thus be just as infective to others, as the person with a very severe and obvious infection.

Q. What kind of physical examination does a doctor have to do to detect genital herpes?

A. In the case of a male patient, a simple inspection of the external genital organs, along with adjacent susceptible areas such as the inner surfaces of the thighs, the groin area, or the buttocks, is usually sufficient to detect any active herpes lesions. Of course the doctor would pay particular attention to any area that the patient identified as painful, irritated, or different from normal.

In the case of a female patient, the physical exam should include a full pelvic examination. This should consist of (1) a careful inspection of the external genital area including the labia, the inner thighs, groin area, and buttocks for any sign of herpes lesions; (2) an examination of the entry to the vagina, the vaginal canal, and the cervix, using a vaginal speculum—an instrument inserted into the vagina to permit the cervix to be examined. A painless scraping of cells from the surface of the cervix for a Pap smear examination would be taken during this part of the exam; and (3) a so-called bimanual pelvic examination in which the physician places one hand on the woman's lower abdomen and introduces two gloved fingers of the other hand into the vagina, thus trapping the uterus and other pelvic organs between his or her two hands to detect any abnormalities or areas of pain. This part of the examination is not a search for genital herpes per se, but for evidence of other possibly more dangerous sexually transmitted infections such as pelvic inflammatory disease or gonorrhea. In a very young, inexperienced, or virginal patient the bimanual part of the exam may be omitted. The vaginal and cervical part of the examination may also be omitted in such a case, or else performed with a special, very narrow vaginal speculum.

Finally, because HSV-1 and HSV-2 infections are often interrelated, the doctor will look for any evidence of cold sores or other herpes lesions on the face and will take a careful history to determine if cold sores have occurred in the past, or if any kind of genital lesion has ever been noted.

Q. Are there any laboratory tests for detecting herpes infections?

A. Yes, several very special laboratory tests can help detect active genital herpes—but these are not the sort of simple, inexpensive, blood-count-and-urinalysis type of exams that might be done as part of a routine physical exam. In fact, most routine lab tests don't provide any useful information at all about genital herpes, except in special cases.

In one of the special tests a patient's blood can be analyzed, not for the virus itself but for the presence of antibodies to herpes simplex viruses. If these antibodies are found in the blood sample, this means that the patient has, at some time in his or her life, been exposed to some herpes simplex virus and because of this exposure the body's immune system has made antibodies against the virus and some of those antibodies still persist. These antibodies may, in fact, remain in the blood for many years after the original infection and many still be present even though the patient has no symptoms whatsoever. The test doesn't tell what type of herpes simplex virus was involved, nor what kind of infection. And it isn't terribly useful in identifying an active genital herpes infection when the antibodies found present might have arisen from a long-forgotten cold sore during childhood.

It is possible to carry this test a little further and type the antibodies to determine whether they are related to type #1 or type #2 herpes simplex viruses, but unfortunately this part of the test is not always accurate since these antibodies often mimic each other, and the test is extremely difficult to perform. Thus this kind of a test is more likely to be valuable as a research tool than as a practical clinical laboratory test to learn about a current herpes infection.

Other tests can be more useful. Often a physician simply cannot tell by inspection whether a lesion in the genital area is caused by genital herpes or not. In such a case the physician can use a cotton swab to collect a sample of cells from the lesion and submit the sample to a laboratory for inoculation into a viral culture. If viruses grow in the culture, a sample from the patient can be added to a tube containing healthy cells growing in an artificial nutrient solution. The viruses can then invade the cells and begin to multiply. Within a few days a trained lab technician can identify the herpes virus. This virus-culturing technique is straightforward enough that most major laboratories can perform the test, although it is likely to be expensive.

Another lab examination, known as the Tzanck smear, can also be helpful. In this test the cells taken from the cotton swab are examined under the microscope using a special stain. Herpes simplex viruses can be identified with the Tzanck test about 60 to 80 percent of the time.

The problem with both the above tests is that sometimes the doctor taking the sample doesn't obtain any live viruses even when active viruses are present—the doctor has no way of being sure—so these two tests may return false negative results, that is, show no evidence of viruses even though viruses in fact are present. Nevertheless, these two tests are extremely helpful, for example, in monitoring a pregnant woman with genital herpes as she approaches the time for her delivery. The tests offer a high probability of success in determining whether the infection is active or not at delivery time. Recently doctors at the National Institutes of Health in Bethesda, Maryland, have reported development of an even better monitoring test: a new high-speed test to detect herpes simplex infections by using a fluorescent dye to help identify viruses. In this new test the genital herpes virus can be detected in just twenty-four hours, compared with the three to ten days required by earlier lab tests. And with refinements, researchers think that the new test time may presently be cut down to as little as four hours.

Finally, as we have noted before, a Pap smear can accurately diagnose genital herpes in about two-thirds of cases. Since the Pap smear misses the other third of cases, it is not a reliable test for genital herpes when the report is negative, but it is useful in confirming the diagnosis when the report is positive for herpes.

Q. Are any of these tests useful to diagnose a recurrent genital herpes infection, or can they only be used to reveal a primary infection?

A. You'll notice that all the tests we have discussed depend upon detecting live, active viruses in the genital region. Since the identical live, active virus that appears in the genital region during a recurrence of genital herpes is present during a primary infection, these tests would be just as valid for recurrent infections as for primary infections.

Q. Is a genital herpes infection ever contagious or spreadable at a time when no symptoms or sores are present?

A. Not ordinarily—but unfortunately, the infection may sometimes be contagious even when there is no evidence of it present at all. Cases have been reported in which an active virus has been isolated from the area of former genital sores that appear to be completely healed. We also know that in certain persons who have repeated cold sores the herpes virus is sometimes present in their saliva even when sores around the mouth are not present. In other words, once a person has contracted a genital herpes infection he or she can never be absolutely 100 percent certain of being noncontagious at any time, although a person is least likely to be contagious at the times when no symptoms or genital sores are present.

Q. Can either one of the herpes simplex viruses cause a primary herpes infection in the genital area?

A. Yes, a person can get completely separate primary herpes cold sores or genital infections from either HSV-1 or HSV-2 at different times. And, as far as is known today, an active HSV-1 infection causing a cold sore can cause a genital herpes infection just as well as an HSV-2 virus can if the HSV-1 viruses are brought in contact with a susceptible genital surface. And it appears that this kind of genital infection from the HSV-1 (cold sore) virus is occurring more and more frequently as a result of more oral-genital sexual contacts practiced today.

Q. Can a genital herpes infection lead to any really serious or life-threatening complications?

A. If you are talking about the infection in otherwise relatively healthy, sturdy, perfectly normal adults, the answer is no—any serious or life-threatening complication would be most exceedingly rare. In two special groups of people, however, herpes simplex can indeed lead to serious and life-threatening complications. These groups are newborn babies, on the one hand, and any individual whose immune system is seriously compromised or weakened for one reason or another and doesn't work properly. Among newborn babies infected with herpes simplex, there is a much greater than normal risk that an infection of cells in the brain by the virus can take place, so-called herpes encephalitis. Newborn babies may also experience a rapidly spreading so-called "miliary" invasion of the virus over all parts of the skin surface, so that the child may succumb to an overwhelming infection that its body simply cannot handle. Similar kinds of widespread herpes infection that cannot be thrown off may

attack immunocompromised persons—persons, for example, who have cancer or who have been given an immuno-
suppressive drug because of a kidney transplant or for other
reasons. In these people herpes simplex infections can present a very real danger. For most people, however, unlike a
truly death-dealing sexually transmitted disease like syphilis,
genital herpes is far more of a nuisance and an irritation than
a life threat.

Q. Does everybody who contracts a genital herpes infection later have recurrences?

A. Not necessarily—in fact, there can be quite a good
deal of variation from person to person. There are a few individuals who have had a genuine, bona fide, laboratory-prov-
en primary infection with genital herpes who simply never
have a recurrence of the infection. That is, when the primary
infection heals, the healing appears to be permanent and no
recurrent symptoms or lesions ever occur. Health authorities
emphasize that these individuals are few and far between,
however. Other individuals, after the healing of the primary
infection, may have only rare and sporadic recurrences, perhaps a year or two apart, or perhaps only one recurrence
after four or five years, etc. On the other hand, there are
some individuals, fortunately comparatively few, who may
have constantly recurring infections, one right after another.

Most individuals fall somewhere between these ex-
tremes. Perhaps the most common pattern is for the person
to have between two and five recurrences per year, some
recurrent episodes more severe than others. Also, most individuals establish a pattern of recurrence that is more or less
predictable or stable. For example, the exact time of a recurrent infection cannot be pinpointed, but a person will know,
from experience, that if he or she has not had a recurrence in
the last, say, three or four months, a recurrence is about
due.

Q. Is there some reason why one person will have recurrences and another person not?

A. No doubt there is a perfectly good reason—something like this is not likely to happen by magic—but we just don't know what the reason is. However, some recent studies suggest strongly that an important part of the reason has to do with an individual body's immune reaction to the herpes virus. We know that the body's immune system does not succeed in eradicating the herpes simplex virus after a primary attack; that virus finds its way up to the spinal nerve ganglia where it "hides out." Some evidence suggests that the virus will stay hiding out and will not reemerge to cause a recurrence as long as the body's immune response to the herpes simplex virus remains strong. According to this way of thinking, it would seem likely that a recurrent attack would occur at some time when the body's immune system is beaten down in some way from some other reason—for example, following a severe illness or during a period of malnutrition. But other evidence suggests that perhaps the herpes virus itself plays a much more active role than this. Some virologists think that the herpes simplex virus itself, in some individuals, may actively beat down or impair the individual's immune system in order to "prepare the way," so to speak, for it to emerge and cause a recurrence of the infection. So far nobody knows whether this or any of these ideas are really true, and this is one of the questions about genital herpes that remains to be answered as more is learned about this odd disease.

Q. Is there any way a person can strengthen his or her immune system in order to prevent recurrent attacks of genital herpes?

A. Not that we know of yet. There is a widespread effort afoot in laboratories all over the world to develop vaccines against herpes simplex virus that might effectively beef up the immune system, but no such vaccines are as yet ready for use. We will discuss this approach to dealing with herpes in more detail in chapter 7.

Q. Are there any good ways to prevent transmission of genital herpes if one sexual partner has an active infection?

A. Yes, the best possible way to prevent transmission of the infection at a time like that is to decline to be a sexual partner. Probably the next best preventive measure would be the male partner's use of a condom or rubber sheath to cover the penis. This would help prevent the spread of the infection regardless of which partner might have the active infection. The use of a condom doesn't *guarantee* protection, but it is certainly better than nothing. Diaphragms, of course, are of no help in protecting against genital herpes, although they may protect against pregnancy. Most health authorities agree that spermicidal jellies are of little or no help in preventing transmission of genital herpes, since these preparations simply don't destroy the virus.

Q. Is it possible that genital herpes can be spread via hot tubs?

A. Three or four years ago a large city Health Department officer reported that there were no proven cases in which genital herpes had been transmitted simply by using a hot tub previously used by someone with an active infection. But more recently I have seen published reports questioning this conclusion, so at present we can only say that nobody really knows. Certainly anyone with an active primary or recurrent infection should be urged to stay out of hot tubs or *any* sort of community bathing facility.

Q. Are there any other possible ways of contracting genital herpes except through sexual contact?

A. Some health authorities think it is possible. It has been shown that herpes simplex virus can survive for at least several hours on cold, dry surfaces, such as toilet seats. Thus it is theoretically possible that an infection could be acquired by contact with contaminated toilet facilities, and one would be well advised to take normal hygenic precautions, like using toilet seat covers, to guard against this remote possibility of contact. There have even been reports of herpes infections being transmitted in the course of contact sports!

Just how important any such nonsexual source of infection may be is something else altogether. Certainly contact with the infection in such ways is pretty unlikely. And indeed, most doctors involved in the treatment of the infection consider these sources negligible.

Q. Lately there has been talk about all kinds of different treatments that one can try against genital herpes. Aside from treatment with acyclovir, are there any other old or new treatment methods that are really effective?

A. Not only are the kinds of treatment you hear about ineffective, but some may be dangerous or damaging as well. Several years ago there was a legitimate medical investigation of a so-called dye and light form of treatment for active genital herpes lesions. In this treatment, the lesions were first painted with an intense red, violet, or purple dye and then the lesions were exposed to fluorescent or incandescent light. The theory was that the dye applied to the surface would permit damaging light waves to penetrate the skin surface and attack the herpes simplex viruses in the deeper layer of cells. Although the early results using this treatment seemed promising, carefully controlled studies of the treatment later demonstrated that it really provided no more help than simply leaving the lesions alone to heal by themselves, and even raised some questions about stimulating cancerous changes in the cells. Since it never proved useful, this form of treatment has now been abandoned.

At one time it was thought that giving a patient with a primary genital herpes infection a smallpox vaccination would help shorten or terminate the infection. We now know that smallpox vaccine is not effective in any way for the treatment of herpes, and is in itself dangerous, expecially when given to a person who has some kind of open skin lesion.

Other forms of treatment, such as painting the lesions with ether, or with DMSO (dimethylsulfoxide, a garlic-smelling solvent that soaks readily through the skin), have proven equally futile. Various treatments involving Vitamin C, Vitamin E, or Vitamin B_{12} have also proven ineffective. Symptoms can, however, be relieved to a limited extent by keeping the active infected area clean and dry and by wearing loose-fitting clothing. Aspirin has no effect on the progress of the infection, but it can often help relieve pain and fever, and does not make anything worse.

Q. I still don't understand where the herpes viruses go to hide in between recurrent infections.

A. Almost all skin areas of the body have nerve fibers reaching to them. These nerve fibers, known as *sensory* or "feeling" nerves, carry sensations of heat, cold, irritation, or pain back to the brain from the surface areas of the body. This communication is carried on through a chain of nerve cells. The nerve fibers in the genital region are actually nothing more than long arms reaching from the skin back to the nerve cell body in the region of the spinal cord. A new nerve cell arm then carries the sensation up the spinal cord toward the brain.

When a genital herpes primary infection subsides in the genital region, the viruses seem able to travel up those nerve arms from the skin surface to the spinal cord and hide in the cell body of the nerve. Nobody knows exactly how they manage to do this, but that's what they seem to do. Nobody knows what happens to the viruses during the dormant or "sleeping" phase while they are lodged inactively in the body of these nerve cells. Some experts believe they become totally inactive and just lie there until something happens to stimulate them; others believe that they may slowly replicate or reproduce themselves in these cells so that a new generation of viruses is ready and waiting to be stimulated later. And nobody knows for sure why they presently come down to cause recurrent infection. They do seem to come down the same nerve fibers, however, because the recurrent infection, when it occurs, usually involves the same general area of surface cells as was affected by the earlier infection. That is, the recurrent infection does not seem to involve some distant area of skin in the region.

Q. Are there any organizations that provide genital herpes patients with ongoing news or counseling about the disease or progress being made against it?

A. Yes, the American Social Health Association, a national nonprofit health foundation, sponsors a special program specifically to assist herpes patients. This program, the Herpes Resource Center, referred to locally as HELP, provides its members with a quarterly newsletter, operates a telephone hot line for information, and organizes local self-help groups. See p. 49 for the address of this organization, or check your telephone directory for a local city number.

Q. If there is no way to cure a genital herpes infection anyway, what's the point of going to a doctor if you think you have contracted the infection?

A. First, it is important to *you* to have a prompt and accurate diagnosis, and a doctor can help you obtain this. Obviously it would be pointless to fret and worry about having a genital herpes infection if in fact you don't have it at all. On the other hand, if you *do* have such an infection, you need to know it so you can begin treatment to help control it and take reasonable and intelligent precautions to prevent spreading it to other people. Second, a doctor can guide you in treatment modalities that are effective in shortening the infection even if the treatment doesn't cure it—the use of Zovirax ointment, for example, in treating a primary herpes infection, or the use of oral acyclovir to help reduce the frequency and severity of recurrent attacks. The doctor can also keep you informed of any new developments in treatment.

Finally, and extremely important, even if the doctor can demonstrate that you do *not* have a genital herpes infection, he or she can help you determine whether or not you have any other sexually transmitted disease and if you do have, can prescribe and monitor treatment for it. This simple point is often overlooked: that the same sexual contact that might expose you to genital herpes can also expose you to certain other, far more dangerous, sexually transmitted diseases. In the following chapter we will discuss some of the diseases that are sometimes mistaken for genital herpes which any sexually active person should know about.

5

OTHER SEXUALLY TRANSMITTED DISEASES

Although genital herpes is a thoroughly unpleasant, painful, and often disruptive sexually transmitted disease, it is not the *only* infective disease that can be transmitted by sexual contact, nor is it by any means the worst. Distasteful and prolonged as genital herpes may be, it does not ordinarily kill people, nor does it cause widespread continuing damage to the body's organs and tissues, as other sexually transmitted diseases can do. Unfortunately some of these other infectious diseases may mimic genital herpes in appearance and symptoms; even when they don't actually resemble genital herpes at all, they are sometimes assumed to *be* genital herpes by a person who has contracted them, and may therefore be neglected when in fact medical help is urgently needed. Gonorrhea and syphilis are by far the most widespread and dangerous of these other sexually transmitted diseases and deserve particular attention here, but other less familiar diseases such as chlamydia infections, lymphogranuloma venereum, chancroid infection, granuloma inguinal, or even common venereal warts should also be mentioned.

GONORRHEA

According to statistics from the Centers for Disease Control in Atlanta, gonorrhea today is by far the most widespread of the sexually transmitted or "venereal" diseases despite the fact that for over forty years we have had some highly effective antibiotics capable of curing it. In fact, during the last ten or fifteen years we have been losing ground against this infection for a very ominous reason: some strains of the bacteria that cause gonorrhea have become vigorously resistant to antibiotic treatment in various parts of the world, and these resistant strains of the germ have been brought back to the United States. One particularly troublesome resistant strain which appeared a few years ago in southeast Asia has been brought home in strength by returning Vietnam war veterans.

Gonorrhea is primarily an infection of the urethra (the tube that carries the urine from the bladder to the outside) in males and the urethra and internal genital tract of females. It has been known to exist for many hundreds of years and today is known by such street names as "G.C.," "the clap," "a strain," or "a dose." The infection is caused by small coffee-bean-shaped germs called *gonococci* or *diplococci* because they always grow together in pairs. They are close cousins to similar germs that cause meningitis.

These bacteria are rather frail organisms that do not survive very long outside the body and are hard to grow in the laboratory. After sexual contact, however, the gonococci find their way up the urethral tube in both the male and the female where they invade cells lining these tubes and set up a highly irritating infection. After contact, the first symptoms appear between thirty-six hours and seven days in the form of a painful irritation and discharge. In the female the bacteria also invade the vagina and in a matter of a few days a thick, yellowish vaginal discharge will appear. In neither case does any surface sore or lesion appear, so the infection does not really resemble genital herpes, but it is very frequently mistaken for it.

If gonorrhea is diagnosed and treated at this early stage of the infection it can be cured in almost every case. In most cases treatment with penicillin, sometimes combined with other common antibiotics, will destroy the infection. Even the new and virulent antibiotic-resistant strains of the infection can be wiped out by treatment with newly developed antibiotics, although the infection may have to be followed up and treated persistently to be sure that it is completely eradicated. The point is that there is no reason for it to remain active if diagnosis and treatment are undertaken promptly. But if the infection is ignored, or inadequately treated, more serious complications can arise.

One thing that may happen is that the gonococci can find their way into the bloodstream and travel to other parts of the body—most notably the joints—and cause a painful and destructive *septic* (infected) *arthritis.* The joints most commonly affected by this complication are the knees, so that a thoroughly destructive and disabling arthritis may occur there, particularly unfortunate because the source of this arthritis may be overlooked and continuing damage to the knee joints may proceed while the physician is treating what he thinks is some other kind of arthritis. Once gonorrheal arthritis is properly diagnosed, the active infective arthritis can be cured by antibiotic treatment, but there is no way that the antibiotic can repair the joint damage that has already been done, and arthritic damage may continue even after the infection has been stopped.

In women, untreated gonorrhea can cause an additional and different kind of complication. The body's natural defenses will fight a gonorrheal infection just as it will fight any other kind of infection, and after a few days or weeks the initial infection will subside. The infection may not be eradicated, however. In such cases the infecting bacteria can work their way up the female genital tract to cause a new acute inflammation involving the uterus, the fallopian tubes, the ovaries, and the supporting structures in the surrounding pelvic area. Often this acute flare-up will be accompanied by fever and acute pelvic or lower abdominal pain so severe that it is sometimes mistaken for acute appendicitis. Doctors often use the rather polite and ambiguous term "pelvic inflammatory disease" or "PID" to describe this condition, because it can in some cases be caused by other bacteria than gonococci, but in most cases it is a complication of gonorrhea.

Again, the body mounts an attack against the organism causing this form of the infection and in most cases it will subside after a few days or weeks. In many women, however, it lingers on in a continuing, smoldering infection that never quite goes away. The worst part of this complication is that the tubes are attacked by the bacteria and often become filled with pus, blocking the passage of the woman's ova down to the uterus. As time passes the tubes become scarred and thickened, resulting in permanent obstruction of the tubes and sterilization. Treatment of the condition at this point may relieve the active infection but in all too many cases the obstructive scarring and damage to the tubes cannot be healed and repaired either naturally or by surgical intervention later. Thus untreated gonorrhea can become one of the major causes of irreversible infertility in women.

SYPHILIS

A second major sexually transmitted infectious disease still rampant today is even more dangerous than gonorrhea. Syphilis accounted for some 33,600 new or early infections reported in the United States in 1982, with an additional 42,000 late-stage cases of the disease identified in the same year. This infection is particularly treacherous because an early infection with syphilis can produce a genital sore or lesion that looks a lot like genital herpes and tends to go away in a few days all by itself, the way a genital herpes lesion does, so that syphilis can be confused with genital herpes and completely missed if the patient doesn't see a doctor. Unfortunately, the syphilis infection doesn't go away when the first lesion heals and disappears. The syphilis organism continues growing inside the body, often for many years, destroying body tissues all that time and doing irreparable damage to the brain, spinal cord, great blood vessels, heart, liver, or other organs. The tragedy of all this is that syphilis can be cured virtually 100 percent of the time with modern antibiotic treatment once it is discovered.

Syphilis is caused by a tiny spiral bacterium or *spirochete* called *Treponema pallidum*. It is transmitted from person to person through sexual contact. The first sign is a small sore usually appearing somewhere on the genitals, differing from the first lesion of genital herpes only in that the syphilis lesion is usually painless. This first or initial sore seems to "heal itself" in a few days. A month or more later a skin rash will appear all over the body, marking a second, more wide-spread stage of infection. This rash also soon disappears. Then, anywhere from two to twenty years later, signs of late-stage syphilis begin to appear, including spinal cord damage, brain cell destruction, weakening and bulging of the wall of the aorta (the great artery in the chest), or destructive lesions in other organs of the body.

The diagnosis of syphilis is not difficult to make once it is suspected. In the early stage, spirochetes in a smear taken from the initial genital sore can be observed under a special *darkfield microscope.* Some months later a blood test known as an STS (serological test for syphilis) begins to show signs of the body's immune reaction to the syphilis organism. This test, which is usually diagnostic of syphilis and nothing else, is the basis of the premarital blood test still required in most states. In addition, most doctors routinely order an STS as part of the lab work included in an ordinary physical examination.

Before antibiotics there was no really effective treatment for syphilis, and a great many people died of the destructive damage caused by late stages of the infection. In the early 1940s, penicillin changed all that; it was found to be almost 100 percent effective in curing syphilis, and it still is. Antibiotic-resistant syphilis is very uncommon. For people who are allergic to penicillin, a variety of other antibiotics are almost equally effective. But unfortunately, curing the active infection does not repair the tissue damage that has already been done by the spirochete. For this reason, early diagnosis and treatment is the only way to be sure of escaping long-term consequences of the infection.

Active syphilis can be transmitted to other persons by sexual contact at the time of the first or initial lesion and again later during the second stage of the disease when the skin rash may be teeming with organisms. What is more, a woman with a syphilis infection who becomes pregnant can pass the organism across the placenta to the developing baby, who may then be born with *congenital syphilis,* with tissue and organ destruction already under way.

TRICHOMONAS

This sexually transmitted infection is really more of a nuisance than a threat, but it can, sometimes, be confused with genital herpes. *Trichomonas vaginalis* is a small, one-celled protozoal organism that grows and reproduces particularly well in a warm, moist, slightly acidic environment such as is found in a woman's vagina. In the infected woman it does not cause any sores or other lesions but produces a rather thin, milky vaginal discharge accompanied by considerable itching quite similar to the itching and burning that can go with genital herpes. The Trichomonas organism can easily be detected on a simple vaginal smear taken and examined in a doctor's office. For a long time this infection was regarded almost exclusively as a "female disease," but today it is recognized that the male can also have the infection, largely symptom-free and unsuspected, and that sex partners can in fact pass the infection back and forth. Under those circumstances it doesn't do very much good to treat and cure the infection in the female, since she is likely to be reinfected the next time she has sexual contact with her partner. Some relatively simple medicines will kill the Trichomonas organism and cure the infection, but treatment should be carried out in both partners simultaneously to have the best chance of getting rid of this nuisance.

CHLAMYDIA

Genital herpes is not the only sexually transmitted disease to be generally recognized recently. Another infection, once better known as "nongonorrheal urethral infection" or NGU, once considered fairly rare, is now known to be quite common. The cause of this infection is *Chlamydia trachomatis,* a very small bacterial germ that behaves something like a cross between a bacterium and a virus. As with gonorrhea, the first symptoms of this infection are an irritation of the urine tube or urethra, complete with pain and burning on urination and a puslike discharge. In women the infection can progress upward to infect the fallopian tubes and cause pelvic inflammatory disease. The difference is that these infections have no gonorrhea organisms present. In the male the infection is focused in the urethra, whereas in the female it seems to center in the cervix. The Chlamydia organism is sensitive to the antibiotic tetracycline or to certain of the sulfa drugs, but both the male and female partners should be treated simultaneously, if possible, because of the problem of back-and-forth reinfection.

Chlamydia trachomatis can cause other problems, too. It is the germ that causes *trachoma,* a chronic eye infection that afflicts multitudes of desert people in North Africa and the Middle East, and native Americans in the southwestern desert of the United States. Certain special subspecies of Chlamydia also cause another sexually transmitted disease, *lymphogranuloma venereum,* an infection that causes swelling and scarring of the lymph nodes in the genital and rectal region. Finally, a different species of Chlamydia causes psittacosis, a dangerous pneumonialike infection acquired from infected parrots, parakeets, and other birds. Fortunately, all these Chlamydia infections respond to tetracycline or sulfa drug treatment.

OTHER SEXUALLY TRANSMITTED DISEASES

Although far less frequent, there are a few other sexually transmitted infections that primarily affect the genital region. One of these, known as *chancroid infection,* is caused by the chancroid bacillus and produces a rather large, painful, craterlike sore in the genital area of either males or females. These lesions can resemble the genital herpes lesions superficially, but there is a big difference: chancroid infection can be cured quickly and completely with appropriate antibiotic therapy. *Granuloma inguinal,* caused by still another bacteria, is a slow-developing infection that causes large areas of infected tissue known as *granulomas* to form deep under the skin in the genital region. This infection also succumbs to long-term antibiotic therapy. Finally, a variety of *papillomaviruses* can cause the formation of so-called venereal warts in the genital and rectal region. These are much the same as warts anywhere else on the body except that they tend to be large and moist and are believed to be transmitted sexually. Usually they can be eradicated, or at least controlled, by the use of various chemicals to dry up or *dessicate* the warts.

There are certain other diseases that are either known or suspected to be transmitted by sexual contact under certain circumstances, but that do *not* affect the genital organs directly and thus are not ordinarily thought of as "sexually transmitted." Two such diseases in particular are in the public eye today and deserve mention here, although neither of them is likely to be confused with genital herpes.

Hepatitis B. This virus primarily attacks the cells in the liver, although the infected person usually has a *viremia*—infective viruses swarming in the blood stream—at some time during his infection. Hepatitis B was originally thought to be transmitted primarily by way of contaminated hypodermic needles and is a notorious problem among individuals using illicit drugs and sharing intravenous drug paraphernalia. The disease is dangerous, with an approximately 10 percent mortality rate, due to widespread destruction of liver cells. However, hepatitis B differs from other kinds of hepatitis in one important way: among those who recover from the infection, some 30 percent continue to carry the live hepatitis B virus in the bloodstream and thus become symptom-free carriers of the infection. Individuals with the active disease, or individuals who have developed this carrier state, are now known to shed the virus from moist body surfaces such as the genital area, so the infection can be transmitted to others by sexual contact. There is no drug or treatment that is effective in curing hepatitis B, but much recent research has been devoted to developing protective vaccines against the virus. Although very expensive, such vaccines are available today, so that persons at particular risk (for example, persons in the same house or the family of an acutely infected person) can be protected from contracting it.

AIDS (Acquired Immune Deficiency Syndrome). This mysterious and deadly disorder has only been recognized for a few years, and even today not a great deal is known about it. For some reason not yet clearly understood, the victim of this disease becomes immune-deficient—that is, an important segment of his or her immune system breaks down and ceases to function. This does not happen as a result of any inherited immune deficiency, but rather is an immune deficiency that is acquired from some source not yet fully understood. Persons with this condition tend to fall victim to a succession of different infections that do not ordinarily even get started in the human body because the normal immune system effectively fights them off. Some victims also develop certain rather obscure kinds of cancer that rarely, if ever, appear in a person with a normal immune system. To date most of the victims of AIDS have either been members or close sexual contacts of certain distinct groups—male homosexuals, active users of illicit intravenous drugs, certain refugees from Haiti who have recently migrated to the United States, or individuals (such as hemophiliacs) who have to use large quantities of blood or blood products over a prolonged period of time.

Since AIDS was first described and reported in the late 1970s there has been a growing suspicion that there was some transmissible agent—some virus, for example—that was attacking people from these groups, possibly because of their sexual habits or because of their contact with blood or blood products. At the present time a particular virus related to certain kinds of leukemia is under intense study as a possible transmitting agent of AIDS, but there is gathering evidence that whatever the transmissible agent is, it can be transmitted by sexual intimacy so that the wife, husband, or partner of an AIDS victim is at high risk of acquiring it.

6

OTHER HERPES INFECTIONS

Genital herpes, caused by the herpes simplex viruses, has certainly stolen the limelight in recent years. None of the other herpes infections are quite so notorious nor so well known. But there are other members of the Herpes Gang of viruses that also cause infections, and some of these infections characteristically affect young people. It will be useful, therefore, to look at some of these other infections now in more detail to see what they can teach us about the behavior of these viruses in general.

THE ZOSTER VIRUS: CHICKEN POX AND BEYOND

Why is it that virologists have grouped a number of quite different herpes viruses together into a single family or class of viruses? One reason is that the kinds of infections these different viruses cause are quite similar in certain ways. As we have seen, the herpes simplex viruses cause primary or "first infection" lesions in the skin at the edge of the lip or in the genital area, and then run and hide away in nerve cells near the spinal cord for long periods of time, only to come out of hiding sometime later and return to the skin areas to cause recurrent infections. Another member of the Herpes Gang does much the same sort of thing in a different way. It too causes a "first infection" in the skin, then runs and hides in nerve cells near the spine and later comes forward to cause a much different kind of skin disturbance.

This unpleasant customer is the *herpes zoster virus* (HZV), also known as the *varicella zoster virus*, considered by some scientists to be the single most infectious microorganism to afflict humankind. Approximately 98 percent of all children suffer a primary HZV infection before they are eight or ten years old. That primary infection is the all-too-familiar childhood rash disease known as *varicella* or ordinary chicken pox.

The virus is spread from person to person by way of respiratory droplets (coughing and sneezing) or by direct contact with the skin rash of the infected person. About two weeks after exposure, the victim comes down with a mild sore throat, a runny nose, and a slight fever—sometimes all so mild that they escape attention. A day or so later, little water blisters or *vesicles* begin appearing on the skin, usually on the face, arms, and body, but sometimes all over, including such unpleasant places as the soles of the feet and between the toes. The blisters begin itching fiercely and soon form a crust which makes them itch even more. Successive waves of new vesicles appear every day or so for seven to eight days. After about eight days the crusted blisters begin to heal and the itching gradually subsides until healing is complete.

Ordinarily these crusted blisters or "pox" will heal without leaving a scar. But if the victim inadvertently introduces skin bacteria into the chicken pox sores by scratching, secondary bacterial infection may develop in some of the lesions, which can result in scars. The vast majority of chicken pox victims, however, recover completely within two weeks without any treatment—and indeed, so far there is no particular treatment that will help speed recovery. For most normal children the infection is little more than an uncomfortable nuisance, although in extremely rare cases a serious complication known as *zoster encephalitis* (inflammation of the brain) has been known to occur. People who somehow miss the disease during childhood and then contract it during adulthood tend to have a much more severe and uncomfortable infection.

If a childhood case of chicken pox were the end of a herpes zoster virus infection, we might consider it mostly an annoyance—and so it was thought to be for many years. Grandma would make the diagnosis from across the room and the victim would be packed off to bed with his or her hands wrapped in mittens to prevent scratching until the disease went away. We now know, however, that even though chicken pox goes away, the virus that causes it does not. Rather, it makes its way up the nerve fibers to find lodging inside nerve cells near the spinal cord where the body's immune system cannot get at it. There the virus lies dormant, in this case usually for *years*, before it reappears.

Nobody knows for certain what causes the HZV to become active again, if and when it does. Many people never do have any further trouble—the virus just lives on in their nerve cells, dormant, for the rest of their lives. But for others, a period of physical or emotional stress may trigger the virus's reawakening. Sometimes the triggering event seems to be a prolonged illness, or malnutrition, or something else that may knock down a person's natural resistance to infection. Recently virologists have come to realize that reawakening of the virus may be triggered by some sudden weakening or breakdown of a person's immune defense system. Thus people in later life who develop a cancer associated with a failure of the body's immune defenses, or a person undergoing kidney transplant, who must take drugs to suppress his or her immune system, are especially vulnerable to renewed infection.

Whatever the triggering incident may be, the virus suddenly stirs itself and starts producing more viruses which travel out along the nerve fibers to the skin, usually in a small limited area on one side of the back or chest, neck or face. There the virus begins producing little clusters of red, inflamed blisters in the skin. At first just itchy, these blisters very soon become painful because they involve the pain nerves to the skin. Within a few days these blisters crust over and heal, sometimes leaving scars in the skin area affected.

The blisters are usually gone within seven or eight days, but the deep-seated aching pain in the area may persist for weeks or months or even longer.

This condition, known as *herpes zoster* or "shingles," is unlike any other herpes infection. If it happens to involve the eye it can cause scarring of the *cornea*, the clear visual window through which we see, and can thus interfere with vision. If it involves the facial nerves, it can cause a temporary paralysis or *palsy* of the muscles of one side of the face—one of the causes of a type of facial paralysis known as *Bell's palsy*. On the neck or back or trunk the infection is mostly a towering nuisance, painful and prolonged. Until very recently there has been no medicine to help with treatment. In most cases the skin lesions quiet down and heal spontaneously within a few days, but the pain may persist for weeks or months after the skin outbreak clears up. What is more, shingles can recur again and again in some people, so that having had it once is no assurance, as it is with chicken pox, that you will never have it again.

For most people herpes zoster virus infections are not terribly important. But a few children every year can suffer such serious complications of chicken pox as *zoster encephalitis* or "brain fever," a form of the infection that can result in brain damage or even death. In addition, early chicken pox or later shingles can be especially dangerous to persons who are immunocompromised—people whose immune protection system is not working properly. Some children are born with an impaired immune system, while others have to take medicines that block the immune systems because of organ transplants or cancer treatment, for example.

Because such people were at very high risk—perhaps life-or-death risk—of infection by the herpes zoster virus, researchers all over the world began working to develop a vaccine that might prevent chicken pox in advance and, too, prevent the virus from lodging in the body to cause shingles later.

In recent years this international research effort has borne fruit. In 1969 the Russian virologist V. I. Iovlev and his co-workers produced a vaccine made from live herpes zoster virus cultures that had been weakened, or attenuated, in the laboratory. This vaccine appeared to confer some degree of protection against chicken pox, but investigators were hesitant to test it too widely in human beings, who were the only available experimental subjects. Then in 1974 the Japanese researcher M. Takahashi developed another live virus vaccine from a different strain of herpes zoster viruses, the so-called Oka strain. This vaccine was widely and successfully tested on children known to have been exposed to chicken pox, with a high rate of prevention. Since then another vaccine has been developed in the United States by researchers at Merck, Sharp and Dohme Pharmaceutical Company. Both the Oka strain vaccine and the Merck vaccine appear extremely promising as protective vaccines, and are undergoing testing in the United States. It is unlikely that either of these vaccines will be certified for general use for several years, but the goal of a successful and safe vaccine is finally in sight.

Meanwhile other research groups have been investigating possible ways to treat patients with acute attacks of shingles, particularly immunocompromised individuals to whom the disease is such a threat. One group has recently used acyclovir administered intravenously to seriously ill patients who have come up with painful shingles infections. This treatment seemed to relieve the pain very dramatically within twenty-four hours and to halt the formation of any new skin lesions within forty-eight hours. The treatment is somewhat limited because the patient has to be hospitalized in order to receive the medicine, but other groups are now testing acyclovir administered by mouth to patients in hopes that it will shorten or terminate shingles attacks. And finally, institutions such as the University of Alabama in Birmingham are testing completely new drugs such as bromovinyl deoxyuridine against HZV in immunosuppressed patients' shingles. This kind of research provides hope that at least this member of the Herpes Gang may be sidelined in the near future.

EB VIRUS AND
THE KISSING DISEASE

For many years doctors were puzzled by a mysterious disease that most often seemed to attack high school–age adolescents, college students, and young adults. Because it behaved like a prolonged infection, and because it often caused large numbers of strange-looking white blood cells with large nuclei to appear in the bloodstream, the disease came to be known by the jaw-breaking name *infectious mononucleosis*, or "infectious mono" for short. Because it often caused enlargement of lymph glands in the neck, under the arms, and elsewhere in the body, it was also sometimes called "glandular fever." Finally, when scientists discovered that the infectious agent, whatever it was, seemed to be spread from person to person in the saliva, it was immediately dubbed "the kissing disease."

Victims of infectious mononucleosis can develop any number of puzzling symptoms. At first the victim feels as if he or she has come down with a severe case of flu, with fever and aching muscles and a feeling of complete exhaustion. Then most victims develop a raw, red sore throat and swollen neck glands. Many, but not all, develop a red, itchy skin rash that often comes and goes in a bewildering fashion. In some patients the liver or spleen or both become tender and enlarged. Almost everybody with the infection soon shows evidence of the strange-looking white cells in the blood, and most people, sooner or later, show laboratory signs of a particular kind of antibody in the blood, suggesting that their body's immune system is fighting off some microscopic invader. Fortunately this infection does not usually cause a very *severe* illness, but what it lacks in severity it makes up for in duration. Often the illness, fever, and feeling of exhaustion go on for weeks, sometimes even months, before full recovery.

What was the cause of this malady? For many years the culprit eluded every effort to pin it down and identify it. Then in 1964 two British virologists, M. A. Epstein and Y. M. Barr, identified a new member of the herpes virus family as the cause of the disease, now known as the Epstein-Barr virus or EBV.

This virus has been the subject of intensive study since its discovery, not only because of its connection with infectious mono, but for its much more serious relationship with certain other diseases. For example, EBV was one of the first viruses to be linked directly to a kind of cancer in humans. When the British surgeon Dennis Burkitt discovered a large number of cases of a peculiar lymph gland cancer among black Africans in a small area of central Africa, he could not understand why so many cases should appear there and almost nowhere else in the world. Investigation proved that many of the cancer cells from patients with Burkitt's lymphoma in central Africa contained Epstein-Barr virus particles. This did not mean that the EB virus necessarily *caused* the cancer (and even today researchers are not sure what the virus particles are doing in those cancer cells) but there does seem to be some sort of link between the virus and the cancer. The same kind of link was later discovered between the EB virus and victims of a form of cancer affecting the nose and throat that occurs quite commonly in southern China but almost nowhere else.

In addition to these suspicious cancer connections, EBV has also been suspected of contributing to a number of other chronic illnesses, particularly a crippling kind of arthritis known as rheumatoid arthritis. In a recent study done at the University of Arizona College of Medicine, researchers reported acute episodes of rheumatoid arthritis in patients who had evidence of active EBV infection, suggesting that

EBV may be involved in acute attacks of rheumatoid arthritis far more commonly than anyone has realized.

Of course, once the Epstein-Barr virus was discovered, the search was on for a vaccine that might be used to prevent infectious mononucleosis or other EBV-related diseases. So far the search has been in vain. No practical, effective vaccine has been developed, nor has any antiviral antibiotic agent yet been discovered to fight EBV. Until such a vaccine is developed there is no way to prevent infectious mono and any person who contracts it must simply wait for it to go away.

CMV AND IMMUNE
DEFICIENT VICTIMS

One last member of the Herpes Gang is little known to most people; in fact, most doctors don't know very much about it or about the infection it causes. This virus bears the name *cytomegalovirus*, from Greek words meaning "enormous cell virus," because certain distinctive giant cells appear in association with the virus in infected areas. Most people find it more comfortable to use the virologists' shorthand and call this virus CMV.

CMV is transmitted from person to person by almost any kind of close contact. The virus can be spread by way of respiratory secretions, saliva, urine, blood, or stool. Once in the body, the virus spreads to virtually all organ systems and can cause any of a variety of different symptoms—fever, liver inflammation, lymph node swelling, pneumonia, sore throat, or even arthritis. For a long time it was thought that the virus attacked only newborn babies and individuals with deficient immune protective systems, since these individuals and small children seemed to be the only ones who became ill. Today, however, virologists suspect that practically everybody contracts a cytomegalovirus infection some time in his or her life, and simply doesn't know it because the infection doesn't produce any recognizable symptoms at all. We do know that some 80 percent of persons forty years of age or older carry antibodies against CMV in their bodies, indicating that there has been some contact or infection with the virus sometime in the past. Yet most of those people have never had an illness that they could identify as a CMV infection.

The ones who are most actively endangered by this virus today are individuals who have the Acquired Immune Deficiency Syndrome or AIDS. These are people who, for reasons unknown, have acquired a severe impairment of their immune protective system and therefore are extremely vulnerable to infections that ordinarily would never have a chance to take hold in their bodies. One of these infections is CMV infection, which appears among these patients with a high degree of frequency. In addition, persons who have had organ transplants and have had to take medicine to block the action of their immune systems are especially vulnerable to CMV infection. At the present time virologists are actively studying this herpes virus in order to learn more about it and the possible dangers it may pose to humans. Experimental antiviral agents and possible vaccines are also under study but these, as yet, are still only in the earliest stages of development.

7

CURBING
THE
HERPES
MENACE

As recently as thirty years ago only a handful of virologists were particularly interested in the Herpes Gang of viruses. At that time, some of this family of viruses hadn't been discovered yet, and those that were known, particularly the herpes simplex twins, were mostly considered to be minor annoyances.

Today we know that the herpes viruses are far more than mere annoyances. They can cause long-lasting, recurring, painful infections that seriously interfere with people's lives. In the case of newborn babies and people with impaired immune systems, they can be fatal. Knowing this, it is not surprising that there are thousands of scientists today working in laboratories all over the world in search of ways to wipe out these menacing viruses and put an end, once and for all, to the infections they cause. But even the most optimistic of these researchers will concede that it is likely to be a long, hard battle before it is won.

Not that it hasn't been done with other dangerous viruses. Thanks to the use of vaccinations and worldwide public health controls, the last case of smallpox anywhere in the world was reported in 1977. Not a single case of new infection by this dangerous virus killer has been reported since. This has certainly been a splendid victory—but we have to remember that the basic weapon to control smallpox, the smallpox vaccination, was first discovered by Edward Jenner in 1796. It was not until 180 years *after* Jenner's discovery that the disease was finally eradicated around the world. Today public health authorities are concentrating their efforts to wipe out another common viral disease, *rubeola* or red measles, using a highly effective measles vaccine. But even though success is within reach, there are still reports of occasional, unexpected outbreaks of measles in the United

States and elsewhere in the world, so the job is not done yet, and nobody can really guess how long it is going to take.

With the herpes viruses, the task may be even tougher. Today we know that these viruses are exceedingly common parasites of humankind—they are literally all over the place. Millions of people in this country alone have had primary infections with the herpes simplex twins. Even more have been attacked by the herpes zoster virus, and we know that people harbor these viruses in their bodies for years after primary infections have occurred. Finally, we know that these viruses are extremely clever about "hiding out" inside living cells so that they cannot be destroyed by protective antibodies floating in the bloodstream. It would be a job of the first magnitude just to prevent new primary infection from these herpes viruses; it will be an even harder job to rid the body of the viruses that have set up housekeeping inside and have every intention of staying there.

In spite of all this, there are two promising approaches that may help us eradicate herpes viruses, sooner or later, or at least to drastically reduce the effects of their parasitic behavior. These approaches involve development of preventive vaccines and the search for antiviral drugs.

HERPES VACCINES
ON THE MARCH

So far there is no safe, effective vaccine that has been fully tested and approved for general use against any of the herpes viruses, but we may not have long to wait. In recent months a number of laboratories have reported progress in developing vaccines against genital herpes, chicken pox, and cytomegalovirus infection. For example, a team of researchers at the University of Washington has been testing a noninfective protein substance derived from HSV-2 as a genital herpes vaccine. These researchers have found that the vaccine causes an immune response in 22 out of 23 test volunteers who have never had genital herpes. That means that the vaccine caused these uninfected people to make their own protective antibodies against the virus so that a primary infection might be prevented if they are ever exposed to the virus. Now further tests are planned on a group of 550 volunteers to determine if the vaccine really *does* prevent genital herpes in a large number of sexually active people.

Another team of researchers, supported by federal funds at a research center at the University of Alabama, is testing a different vaccine originally developed at the University of Chicago. This vaccine was made with the help of genetic engineering techniques that, in simple terms, allowed researchers to develop a new but noninfective strain of herpes simplex viruses. This vaccine has been successful in laboratory trials, and testing on human subjects should soon get under way. Still another laboratory in England is busily working on another form of genital herpes vaccine.

In the search for an effective genital herpes vaccine, *genetic engineering* has been playing an increasingly important role. Until very recently virtually all vaccines have been made by taking viruses, bacteria, or other microbes and either killing them or weakening them to the point that they can't cause disease but are still potent enough to trigger the body to build up an immunity to disease. The famous Sabin polio vaccine, for example, is nothing more than a weakened or "tamed" polio virus incapable of causing paralytic polio but still active enough to signal the body's immune system to defend against the normal disease-causing polio virus.

Unfortunately, making vaccines from such weakened microbes can take years of tedious effort and even then may not work. But genetic engineering has enabled researchers to get around such problems. In the case of the herpes simplex viruses, instead of trying to grow the viruses and then find ways to weaken them, scientists have been able to reach inside the viruses and remove the genes responsible for certain special surface proteins or antigens on the viruses. These genes are then inserted into harmless bacteria, which begin to produce the antigen alone without any of the dangerous infective qualities of the virus.

Now researchers are trying to piece together the right antigens grown in this fast, highly purified form to produce the most effective vaccine. One such herpes simplex vaccine is in an advanced stage of development by a small biotechnology company, Molecular Genetics, Incorporated, working in partnership with the Lederle Division of American Cyanamid Company. Still another such vaccine is being developed by Merck & Company, the big drug maker. Years of testing may be required, however, before these new vaccines can be approved for general use in humans.

Much closer to general use is the Oka strain varicella virus vaccine that we mentioned in chapter 6, which may prove to be a safe, effective vaccine to protect children against chicken pox. That vaccine has already had extensive human testing and will probably be generally available soon. In addition, researchers at the University of Pennsylvania and the University of Minnesota, working in collaboration, have begun testing in humans a new vaccine against cytomegalovirus infection—a vaccine that would be a particular boon to organ transplant patients and those whose immune defense systems are not working properly.

When will any of these vaccines be available for general use? And in particular, when will a protective vaccine against genital herpes be available? Nobody knows for sure. Researchers must first make sure that any such vaccine is actually effective in preventing herpes infection, and perhaps more importantly, they must be sure that the vaccine is absolutely safe. Probably the earliest that any of these vaccines can be approved for widespread use will be sometime late in the 1980s or early in the 1990s, except for the chicken pox vaccine which may be ready sooner. But one thing seems certain: sooner or later such vaccines will certainly become available.

<h2 style="text-align:center">CLOSING THE DOOR ON
THE HERPES VIRUSES</h2>

The other battlefield in the fight against genital herpes and other herpes virus infections involves the search for powerful and effective antiviral drugs—antibiotics or chemicals that will help the body's natural defenses destroy these viruses and prevent their reproduction in the body's cells.

In chapter 3 we talked at some length about acyclovir and its action against genital herpes. In many ways this drug is an important milestone, one of the first antiviral drugs ever found effective in treating and controlling an established virus infection that is already going on in the body. Other drugs, such as *amantidine,* can *prevent* some people from getting hepatitis B infections, or reduce the severity of the infections, but it cannot stop the virus once it has actively infected the body.

Acyclovir, on the other hand, can change the whole pattern of a primary genital herpes infection because it can prevent the viruses in the skin lesions from reproducing. Unfortunately, its action in the form of an ointment for surface application is very limited. The drug doesn't kill the genital herpes virus, nor does it eradicate it from the body. Doctors are not yet sure that the drug helps at all in recurrent infections when used in the ointment form, and it is clumsy and painful to apply. Recently, however, experimental use of acyclovir in other dosage forms—in pills to be taken by mouth, for example, or in injectable form for administration intravenously—has proven very promising. In 1983 doctors at the University of Washington Herpes Research Clinic in Seattle, working in cooperation with researchers at the University of California at San Diego, tested oral acyclovir on patients with known genital herpes to see if the drug taken by mouth would have any effect on recurrent infections, when compared with other patients who received only dummy pills or *placebos.* While the patients taking placebos had no change in frequency or severity of recurrent episodes of their genital herpes, the patients taking acyclovir by mouth every day had over 50 percent fewer recurrences, and the recurrences that they had were of shorter duration and had fewer viruses in the recurrent lesions. Furthermore, the medicine taken on a daily basis had very few undesirable side effects. In 1985 the FDA approved the use of oral acyclovir for treatment of recurrent genital herpes, and the drug is now available. How successful it may be in widespread use, however, remains to be seen.

In another study, patients with primary or first episodes of genital herpes were given acyclovir intravenously for a five-day period. The pain and discomfort of the primary lesions were found to be shortened by as much as five days, and the primary lesions healed twelve days sooner than expected in the patients with the intravenous drug therapy.

Clearly acyclovir is a useful drug in combatting genital herpes even though it cannot be called a cure. The job now facing researchers is to figure out which dosage form of acyclovir should be given to which patients to accomplish the most long-term good. Oral and intravenous dosage forms of the drug have also been found to be helpful in treating herpes zoster infections, particularly chicken pox in immunocompromised children and severe shingles in older patients. There is still one growing concern about the use of this drug, however: there is increasing evidence that the more widely acyclovir is used, the more risk there is that drug-resistant strains of the herpes simplex viruses will develop. Unless some way is found to get around this problem, the usefulness of the drug will be seriously limited in the future. Researchers hope that the development of resistant strains of virus will not be swift or widespread, and that further research into this kind of antiviral drug may produce a new, improved, "second generation" acyclovir that may do a much better job of halting the virus than the drug that is now available.

Other drugs are also being studied for use against the herpes simplex twins as well as other herpes viruses. In fact, at the present time, a broad coalition of universities in the United States and Canada are collaborating in an effort to find other antiviral agents to use against the herpes viruses. One agent, *vidarabine,* has been found to be effective in blocking viral reproduction in patients suffering from a rare but deadly form of herpes simplex infection of the brain known as *herpes simplex encephalitis* or "brain fever." *Interferon,* a natural antiviral substance produced by the body's white blood cells and other tissues, is being studied for its effect against all kinds of herpes virus infections and a new drug called *bromovinyl deoxyuridine* is being tested against herpes zoster virus as a possible means of treating chicken pox and shingles. And at St. Mary's Hospital Medical School in London another drug called *arildone* has been shown to have the effect of preventing virus reproduction in cytomegalovirus cultures in the laboratory, suggesting that it might block human infection caused by that virus, and possibly be useful in treating genital herpes as well.

Fortunately, researchers today know much more about viruses than ever before, and in recent years they have learned a very great deal about the Herpes Gang. Years ago the search for weapons against dangerous viruses was a hit-or-miss, happenstance matter of wandering around through half knowledge until something turned up. No more is this true. Virus researchers today know exactly what they are looking for and exactly where to look. There is good reason to hope that within the next few years we will be very close to the goal of wiping out the Herpes Gang or at least keeping it under better control than ever before.

INDEX